Salesforce Anti-Patterns

Create powerful Salesforce architectures by learning from common mistakes made on the platform

Lars Malmqvist

BIRMINGHAM—MUMBAI

Salesforce Anti-Patterns

Group Product Manager: Alok Dhuri
Publishing Product Manager: Harshal Gundetty
Senior Editor: Ruvika Rao
Technical Editor: Pradeep Sahu
Copy Editor: Safis Editing
Project Coordinator: Manisha Singh
Proofreader: Safis Editing
Indexer: Subalakshmi Govindhan
Production Designer: Ponraj Dhandapani
Developer Relations Marketing Executives: Deepak Kumar and Rayyan Khan
Business Development Executive: Puneet Kaur

First published: December 2022

Production reference: 1171122

Published by Packt Publishing Ltd.
Livery Place
35 Livery Street
Birmingham
B3 2PB, UK.

ISBN 978-1-80324-193-7

www.packt.com

To Damiana, Ada, and Pino. To my mother, Inger Bejder, and the memory of my father, Finn Malmqvist.

– Lars Malmqvist

Contributors

About the author

Lars Malmqvist has spent the past 13 years working as an architect and CTO within the Salesforce ecosystem. He has worked on over 40 Salesforce implementations, ranging from simple out-of-the-box scenarios to advanced, bespoke, multi-cloud solutions for large global brands. He is a 29-time certified Salesforce CTA with degrees in anthropology, mathematics, and technology management, an MBA from the University of Cambridge, and a Ph.D. in computer science from the University of York. Currently, he is a partner at Implement Consulting Group.

I would like to thank my wife, Damiana, for her undying support and my children, Ada and Pino, for their constant inspiration.

About the reviewers

Ashvin Bhatt is an enterprise architect, technical writer, trainer, and speaker with over 11 years of experience with the Salesforce platform working on various clouds. He has trained over 600 people on Salesforce through various initiatives. He is a certified Application Architect and holds a wealth of experience with various Salesforce products. Ashvin is the co-organizer of the Salesforce Architect Summit and has been a speaker at various events, such as Dreamforce and TDX. He has worked in a variety of domains such as high tech, advertising, manufacturing, healthcare, insurance, and pharma, to name a few. He believes in sharing his knowledge through community-led initiatives to help foster learning and innovation.

Rafael Gutiérrez Castillo is a Salesforce architect with multi-cloud implementation experience. With more than 10 years of working experience, he started his career in the education industry, developing leadership programs for university students.

He has worked in different positions within the Salesforce ecosystem, as a business consultant, tester, solution consultant, and solution architect.

Working as an associate manager at Accenture, he designs solutions that bridge the gap between business processes and technology and advises companies on their digitalization and transformation journeys. Being the proud owner of 24 Salesforce certificates, he is passionate about automation processes, solution design, process management, innovation, and leadership.

Table of Contents

3

How Not to Get Confused about Security   41

4

What Not to Do about Data   63

Part 2: Solution Anti-Patterns

5

Unpicking Solution Architecture Troubles   83

6

Keeping Integration Straight   113

Part 3: Process and Communication Anti-Patterns

7

Keeping the Development Life Cycle from Going off Track   139

8

Communication without Mistranslation   155

9

Preface

Salesforce is the world's leading enterprise systems platform. This is a position it has reached over the last decade, with its scope having grown from its roots in sales and customer service to encompass a wide range of business domains.

However, as Salesforce has grown, so have the complexities of the technological environments that contain it. And with that growing complexity, a number of common mistakes have emerged that often end up derailing Salesforce projects in a number of interesting ways.

These mistakes are what we will learn to call anti-patterns and investigate in a structured manner in this book. There are quite a few books on Salesforce architecture already available on the market today, but they all approach the subject from a normative view, grounded in good practice.

In this book, we flip that perspective around. We look at bad practices that commonly occur in Salesforce projects, and that, in fact, can seem like a good idea at the time you make the decision.

By doing that, we see what happens when things don't go to plan – when you don't make the right call, and your solution suffers as a consequence. That gives a great background for us to review key architectural concepts and good practice as it applies across a range of scenarios.

In this book, you will get information structured into the seven domains of the **Certified Technical Architect (CTA)** exam roadmap. That way, while all the information is based on real-world examples, you will also be able to directly apply it in your journey to becoming a CTA, should that be a path you are on or are considering.

Who this book is for

This book is for anyone who has a position of responsibility in a Salesforce implementation and wants to see it avoid the common mistakes that plague many projects. While the primary audience is architects or aspiring architects, it will also be of value for project managers, business analysts, functional consultants, and executives overseeing Salesforce projects.

What this book covers

Chapter 1, Why You Need to Understand Salesforce Anti-Patterns, starts by explaining what anti-patterns are by going through a number of different definitions and ways of looking at them. You will then learn how they can help you deepen your understanding of architecture by understanding how these common mistakes are made and how they can seem like a good idea at the time. We then finish the chapter by understanding the book and the ways in which you can approach the content.

Chapter 2, How Not to Mess Up Your System Architecture, guides you through common anti-patterns relating to the systems landscape, the mix of systems you use in your solution, and how they can be combined. We will start by looking at anti-patterns at the highest level that describe problems around the composition and scoping of systems. Then we will look at anti-patterns that create highly coupled and brittle system landscapes, after which we will look at anti-patterns around selecting the right systems to include. The chapter will end with a review of the key takeaways for real life and the CTA Review Board.

Chapter 3, How Not to Get Confused about Security, includes anti-patterns related to securing your Salesforce org. It starts by reviewing a key anti-pattern around the shared security model that is integral to Salesforce. Then we will look at anti-patterns that can occur when you mistake other things for security. We will continue to look at how not to make a mess of your sharing model and once again finish up with a review of the takeaways.

Chapter 4, What Not to Do about Data, contains anti-patterns related to data architecture, modeling, and governance. We will start by looking at what goes wrong when you don't design with Salesforce's object model in mind. Then we will look at some of the common governance disasters that can happen around data. From there, we will look intently at data synchronization and the ways in which it can go wrong, and finish up with takeaways for life and the CTA Review Board.

Chapter 5, Unpicking Solution Architecture Troubles, covers anti-patterns related to your solution architecture. We will start by looking at anti-patterns related to your choice of solutions. Then we will look at things that can go wrong when you do functional design. Thirdly, we will look at some particular anti-patterns that affect customizations, first at the conceptual level and then at the code level. We will end the chapter by summarizing the key takeaways.

Chapter 6, Keeping Integration Straight, looks at anti-patterns around your integrations with other systems. The first part of the chapter looks at anti-patterns around the integration landscape and integration patterns. The second part looks at what can go wrong in the design and use of interfaces, and the third zooms in on problems with particular integration styles such as event-based architectures and batch transfers. As always, we end the chapter by distilling the key takeaways.

Chapter 7, Keeping the Development Life Cycle from Going off Track, looks at anti-patterns related to areas such as development process, governance, and DevOps. We will start by tackling a few significant process-level anti-patterns and then move on to a couple that deal with DevOps and packaging. Finally, we will tackle a common and very unfortunate anti-pattern related to testing. At the end of the chapter, we will summarize the key takeaways for real life and the CTA Review Board.

Chapter 8, Communication without Mistranslation, deals with anti-patterns centered around the way you communicate architecture to different audiences. The first part relates to anti-patterns that relate to information control. Then we look at a few anti-patterns that relate to the clarity of your communication. Thirdly, we look at an anti-pattern specifically about the way you create architectural artifacts. As we've been doing all along, we will end the chapter by summarizing our key takeaways.

Chapter 9, Conclusion, gives a broad overview of the content of the book, including the overarching takeaways from the preceding chapters. It then explains how you can use the anti-pattern method and perspective in your own work to improve your architecture skills. Finally, it gives you pointers on how you can go to progress further in this direction.

To get the most out of this book

This book is intended for anyone who has a stake in making Salesforce projects successful. While some of the technical chapters will make assumptions about general technical knowledge and experience, the only real precondition is a general knowledge of and interest in the Salesforce platform.

Download the color images

We also provide a PDF file that has color images of the screenshots and diagrams used in this book. You can download it here: `https://packt.link/xGcuB`.

Conventions used

There are a number of text conventions used throughout this book.

Any command-line input or output is written as follows:

```
@isTest
class dummyTest{
  static testMethod void notRealTest(){
    //assume A is a class with two methods
    A aInstance = new A();
      aInstance.methodA();
    aInstance.methodB();
    //nothing is done to test anything
  }
}
```

Bold: Indicates a new term, an important word, or words that you see onscreen. For instance, words in menus or dialog boxes appear in **bold**. Here is an example: "When building custom solutions on Salesforce, you will generally be using Apex, an object-oriented language closely related to Java. That means you should be following good **object-oriented analysis and design (OOAD)** practices if you are proposing to build anything non-trivial on the platform."

> **Tips or important notes**
> Appear like this.

Get in touch

Feedback from our readers is always welcome.

General feedback: If you have questions about any aspect of this book, email us at customercare@packtpub.com and mention the book title in the subject of your message.

Errata: Although we have taken every care to ensure the accuracy of our content, mistakes do happen. If you have found a mistake in this book, we would be grateful if you would report this to us. Please visit www.packtpub.com/support/errata and fill in the form. Any errata related to this book can be found at https://github.com/PacktPublishing/Salesforce-Anti-Patterns.

Piracy: If you come across any illegal copies of our works in any form on the internet, we would be grateful if you would provide us with the location address or website name. Please contact us at copyright@packt.com with a link to the material.

If you are interested in becoming an author: If there is a topic that you have expertise in and you are interested in either writing or contributing to a book, please visit authors.packtpub.com.

Share Your Thoughts

Once you've read *Salesforce Anti-Patterns*, we'd love to hear your thoughts! Scan the QR code below to go straight to the Amazon review page for this book and share your feedback.

https://packt.link/r/1-803-24193-4

Your review is important to us and the tech community and will help us make sure we're delivering excellent quality content.

Download a free PDF copy of this book

Thanks for purchasing this book!

Do you like to read on the go but are unable to carry your print books everywhere?

Is your eBook purchase not compatible with the device of your choice?

Don't worry, now with every Packt book you get a DRM-free PDF version of that book at no cost.

Read anywhere, any place, on any device. Search, copy, and paste code from your favorite technical books directly into your application.

The perks don't stop there, you can get exclusive access to discounts, newsletters, and great free content in your inbox daily

Follow these simple steps to get the benefits:

1. Scan the QR code or visit the link below

https://packt.link/free-ebook/978-1-80324-193-7

2. Submit your proof of purchase
3. That's it! We'll send your free PDF and other benefits to your email directly

Part 1: Technical Anti-Patterns

Part 1 will teach you how to identify and mitigate anti-patterns in the technical domains of system architecture, data architecture, and security architecture.

This part has the following chapters:

Why You Need to Understand Salesforce Anti-Patterns

Salesforce anti-patterns tell us about the kinds of systematic mistakes that make their way into many Salesforce projects, mistakes that can even seem like a good idea at the time of implementation but end up having serious drawbacks in the long run. We will learn the most common of these mistakes and how to think about them throughout this book. However, to do so, we must first really understand what anti-patterns are and how understanding them can help us architect and design better systems.

In consequence, this chapter will start by explaining what anti-patterns are by going through a number of different definitions and ways of looking at them. You will then learn how they can help you deepen your understanding of architecture by knowing how these common mistakes are made and how they can seem like a good idea at the time. We then finish the chapter by explaining the book and the ways in which you can approach the content.

In this chapter, we're going to cover the following main topics:

- Understanding anti-patterns

- Where do anti-patterns come from?

- How can anti-patterns deepen your architecture skills?

- Learning about anti-patterns from an example

Understanding anti-patterns

Most developers and architects will be familiar with the concept of a pattern – a good solution to a recurring problem within an architectural domain described in a formalized and reusable way. Some classic examples include the following:

- **Singleton**: A software design pattern that limits the number of instances of a given type to one.

- **Fire-and-forget**: An asynchronous integration pattern that sends off a message from a computational context and proceeds without waiting for a response.

- **Model-View-Controller (MVC):** An architectural pattern that divides an application into three tiers with specifically defined responsibilities:

  I.   First, a model maintains the state of the application and is responsible for any changes to data

  II.   Second, a view shows a particular representation of that model to an end user via some interface

  III. Third, a controller implements the business logic that responds to events in the user interface or changes in the model and does the necessary mediation between the view and the model

This pattern is shown in the following diagram:

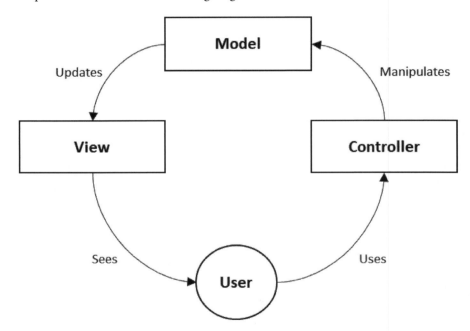

Figure 1.1 – MVC pattern diagram

Patterns such as these have been defined at many levels of abstraction and for many different platforms.

References

You can look at the following resources to get a good introduction to the various patterns that one can apply from a Salesforce perspective.

The integration patterns guide lists all the main patterns to use when designing Salesforce integrations: `https://developer.salesforce.com/docs/atlas.en-us.integration_patterns_and_practices.meta/integration_patterns_and_practices/integ_pat_intro_overview.htm`. In a Salesforce world, this may be the most commonly referenced set of patterns as they are ubiquitous for integration design.

The book *Apex Design Patterns* from Packt, by Anshul Verma and Jitendra Zaa, provides patterns at the software design level and the concrete code level for the Apex language.

The Salesforce Architects site, while new, contains a range of patterns across domains, from code-level specifics to reference architectures and solution kits to good patterns for selecting governance: `https://architect.salesforce.com/design/#design-patterns`.

The point is that we have lots of good patterns to choose from on the Salesforce platform, many that are provided by Salesforce themselves, others by the wider community. Many patterns that apply to other platforms are also relevant to us and we learn much by studying them.

But this is a book about anti-patterns, not patterns. So why am I starting with a discussion about patterns? It turns out that the two are nearly inseparable and originate in the same tradition. Understanding anti-patterns, therefore, begins with an understanding of what a pattern is. Indeed, one common form of anti-patterns is a *design pattern* that has been misapplied. We will explore this in the next section.

From pattern to anti-pattern

The design pattern movement in software architecture originates from the work of Christopher Alexander, an architect whose job was to design buildings rather than systems. In his work *The Timeless Way of Building*, he introduced a pattern template for physical architecture that consisted of a name, a problem statement, and a solution in a standardized format.

The rhetorical structure provided by the Alexandrian template was rapidly adopted by architects of a different kind, the ones that build software. They recognized the power of a standardized way to describe problem-solution sets for communicating good practice. With the publication of the classic Gang of Four book, *Design Patterns: Elements of Reusable Object-Oriented Software*, the use of patterns became mainstream within software development and remains so to this day.

The research on patterns inspired an incipient community of practitioners and researchers in software engineering to think about failure modes of software systems analogously to how design patterns were being used. This happened over an extended period of time, and it isn't possible to point to anyone in the anti-patterns movement that can be seen as the genuinely foundational figure.

However, many research papers on the topic start with the definition given by Andrew Koening in the Journal of Object-Oriented Programming in 1995. This definition says that an anti-pattern is very similar to a pattern and can be confused for one. However, using it does not lead to a solution, but instead has negative consequences.

That definition captures much of the essence and can be usefully combined with the following thoughts from Jim Coplien, another early pioneer. He thought that good patterns in and of themselves were not sufficient to define a successful system. You also have to be able to show that anti-patterns are absent.

In a nutshell, then, an anti-pattern is a pattern that occurs in unsuccessful software systems or projects that can look superficially like a good solution but in practice gets you into trouble. Some common anti-patterns that have been around for ages and are still relevant include the following:

- **Stovepipe**: A system or module that is effectively impossible to change because of how its interfaces are designed. See the following diagram for an illustration:

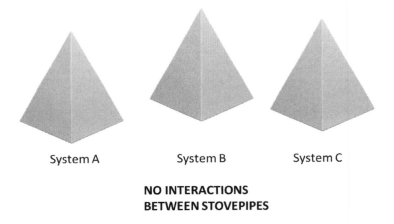

System A   System B   System C

**NO INTERACTIONS
BETWEEN STOVEPIPES**

Figure 1.2 – The Stovepipe anti-pattern

- **Blob**: A design where a single class effectively encapsulates all the business logic and functionality, leading to major maintenance headaches.
- **Intensive coupling**: A design that uses an excessively large number of methods from another class or module in implementing a feature, leading to a deep dependency that is hard to understand or change.

We'll dig into all these anti-patterns from a Salesforce perspective in later chapters, underscoring the unfortunate fact that Salesforce, while a great platform, is still a software system prone to the kind of mistakes that have plagued software systems for decades. If this were not the case, then, of course, there'd be no need for this book or, for that matter, for Salesforce architects.

Having discussed the historical origins of anti-patterns, we will now discuss how they arise in the real world.

Where do anti-patterns come from?

Anti-patterns tend to arise again and again because the circumstances that drive technology projects into trouble are at least somewhat predictable. Equally predictable are the responses of people put into those situations and as people in tough spots frequently make the same bad decisions, we get systematic patterns to study.

Generally speaking, the most important thing to remember about anti-patterns is that they seem like a good idea at the time. They aren't simply bad practices that someone should know better than to apply. You can make a reasoned argument that they should lead to good or at least acceptable outcomes when applied.

Sometimes the decision to apply an anti-pattern is down to inexperience, and sometimes it is down to desperation. But as often as not, it is down to experienced professionals convincing themselves that in this case, doing what they're doing is actually the right call or that this situation really is different.

We will try to reflect this diversity of origins in the examples we show throughout this book. However, to do this, we first need to show how we will present the examples in a consistent way to enable learning.

An anti-pattern template

One of the key characteristics of both patterns and anti-patterns is that they are written using a recognizable template. Many templates have been suggested over the course of the years, some more elaborate than others.

The template we will use in this book contains the bare bones that recur in nearly all existing anti-pattern templates. However, we do not include a great number of optional elements. Most additional elements that are included in other templates serve to ease categorization or cross-referenceability. Those are highly desirable elements to have when creating a searchable catalog of patterns or anti-patterns but are less useful in a printed book. Therefore, we omit them and instead include the following elements:

- **Name**: An easy-to-remember moniker for the pattern that serves to identify it uniquely and help discourse among architects.

- **Type**: In this book, we categorize our anti-patterns by the domain from the **Certified Technical Architect (CTA)** review board examination that they are relevant to. This is both to help people on the CTA journey, but also because this is a familiar typology for Salesforce architects.

- **Example**: We will introduce each anti-pattern by giving an example of how it might occur. The examples will be fictional but grounded in real-world events. This will frame the anti-pattern and give you an immediate understanding of the issues involved before delving deep into the nuts and bolts.

- **Problem**: This section describes more formally the problem or problems that the anti-pattern purports to solve. These are the real issues that the anti-pattern is meant to be a solution for, although using it in practice will turn out to be a bad idea.

- **Proposed solution**: How the anti-pattern claims to solve the problem described in the previous section and how that can be tempting to believe given certain circumstances.

- **Results**: In the results section, we outline what results you can expect from applying the anti-pattern along with its main variations. We go into the detail of why this is a bad solution, although it might look good at the outset.

- **Better solutions**: The final section in the template will tell you what to do instead when faced with the problem that is the basis for the anti-pattern. Not all problems have easy solutions, but you can generally do better than applying an anti-pattern.

Now that we have an understanding of what anti-patterns are and how they are going to be structured in this book, we will move on to explaining how you, as an architect, can improve your skills by using them to learn.

How can anti-patterns deepen your architecture skills?

While a theoretical understanding of what patterns and anti-patterns are and how they might generally be helpful is great, you are no doubt looking for more from this book than just a theoretical discussion.

In this section, we will go through the value of learning from mistakes, both your own and other people's, and show you how we are going to use anti-patterns to sharpen your architecture chops in the context of a concrete example.

How great architects learn from mistakes

We work in an industry where failure is a normal occurrence. The Standish Group CHAOS report, which is the most commonly cited source on these matters, in 2020 estimated that 66% of all technology projects globally ended in partial or complete failure.

This is a little bit better than when I started my career more than 20 years ago. Then, the figure stood in the low 70s. However, while things have improved, they have only improved a little bit, despite agile development, cloud computing, artificial intelligence, and great software platforms such as Salesforce.

This is disheartening, but only proves the point of one of my personal heroes, Fred Brooks, that *"The complexity of software is an essential property, not an accidental one,"* which unfortunately means that we will never find a silver bullet to solve all problems in software architecture and design. Instead, we are faced with the hard work of learning how to manage this complexity in a reasonable way. To do so is the principal job of an architect.

It stands to reason that in an area with high failure rates and irreducible complexity, we need to have good rules and guidelines to keep us on the right path. That is what patterns and best practices are for. They are indispensable, but they are not enough.

To become great at our profession and to be able to design software that bucks the industry trend, we need not just learn from our own failures but also from the vast repository of failed projects and bad practices we see all around us.

That usually isn't hard to do. Many times, when the architect is brought into a project, it is because there is already an issue to fix. Using these occurrences as learning opportunities and analyzing them with that view in mind can be greatly rewarding.

However, there is a step further to go in this direction, which is what anti-patterns offer. They encompass the ways in which things frequently go wrong in a way that allows both post-hoc learning and also real-time intervention.

The thing is that while projects go wrong, they don't do so randomly. There are systematic patterns that repeat time and again. Learning how things go wrong in systematic ways can give you an entirely new set of responses in your toolbox that you can deploy to help make your project one of the 34% that don't fail.

We will start that learning journey with an explanatory example.

An example: The Hero anti-pattern

There is no better way to start learning than using an example. We won't have the chance to cover many general management-level anti-patterns in this book, so I will use one of the classics in this genre to show you how the template works and how to read it to get the most out of it.

First, we will present the anti-pattern and then provide an analysis of what we can learn from it.

Hero (development life cycle and deployment planning)

Tom is the project manager for a large greenfield Salesforce implementation in the manufacturing industry working with Sales and Service Cloud for 2,000 users. The project is meant to be quite simple, a basic MVP to get the platform off the ground, and that is how it has been scoped and staffed. The project is meant to go into full production after six months with four months of implementation followed by test, training, rollout, and hypercare.

The first three months of implementation fly by and everything on the project management dashboard stays green. The team makes steady progress and relations with the external consultancy that is helping provide specialist resources remain good.

However, when Tom delivers the first round of business reviews, things start to change quickly. It turns out that a lot of detailed requirements have been missed from the initial scope and that many edge cases aren't covered by the current configuration. The feedback from the business is that they won't be able to go live with the system unless a large list of additional functionality is included.

Tom goes to the steering committee to ask for more budget and a scheduled increase to accommodate the business demands. The steering committee grants the request for an increased budget but tells him that the schedule is immovable. He must find a way to get it done within the current timeline.

Tom replans the project from the ground up. He can just make it all fit by compressing the testing and cutover plan if he adds some new resources from the external partner and asks for some overtime from his existing team. He sends out the new plan to the team along with a rousing email calling on everyone to rise to the challenge.

Over the course of the next month, the project slips again, and Tom's new plan is looking less and less likely to succeed. It's not that anything big goes wrong, but lots of little things just aren't completed on time or require rework because of misunderstandings. In particular, the new consultants he has brought in from the external partner seem to make a lot of basic mistakes.

Tom calls his boss, the Senior Director for IT, to tell him about the situation and ask for help in getting an extension to the schedule. She tells him that the schedule has been committed to the board of directors of the company and that heads will roll if it is not met. This is the time for the team to pull out all the stops and get it done, she says.

Tom goes back to his team to relay the news and once again calls for everyone to give it everything to get things over the line. Unfortunately, most people are already working as hard as their situations allow. In addition, relations with the external partner have soured and they are not willing to put in additional hours without additional funding, which Tom does not have in the budget.

There are some bright spots, however. In particular, two young members of the technical staff, Kayleigh and Negash, prove willing to go above and beyond in order to get things done. Over the final month of delivery, they work 24/7 on the project with Tom cheering them on.

Figure 1.3 – The dangerous feeling one might have when engaging in the Hero anti-pattern

Between the two of them, they manage to clear away enough of the new features and change requests during the final stretch that Tom feels growing confidence that he will be able to meet enough of the requests for the project launch to not be a disaster. There will be exceptions, but he can find a way of managing those later. As long as the impending go-live goes well, the project can still succeed.

However, **User Acceptance Testing (UAT)** throws a spanner in the works as major quality issues are discovered. The steering committee holds a crisis meeting that ends up concluding that the go-live will have to be postponed for a week. The team will have to work flat out during this period to fix the issues.

While everyone pitches in, the responsibility falls disproportionately on Kayleigh and Negash, who are both starting to show the strain of the continuous effort. Tom gives them encouragement at every chance and singles them out for public praise. He also promises them a cash bonus and extra holidays when the project is done.

The day for retesting arrives and while many issues have been fixed satisfactorily, there are quite a few remaining issues, including a good number that had previously been fixed and are now recurring.

The steering committee holds another crisis meeting and they take the decision to go ahead with the launch despite the issues. These issues will need to be fixed during the hypercare period, but they can be tolerated for a short amount of time.

The next few weeks of Tom's, Kayleigh's, and Negash's lives happen in a blur of constant motion. They are pulled from escalation to escalation as issues occur, are fixed, and reoccur. Kayleigh and Negash start buckling under the pressure, but with no alternative resources knowing the configuration, they are effectively forced to carry on.

Eventually, the issues settle down. The important bugs are fixed, the business puts in place manual workarounds for the things that were missed, life starts to get back to normal. Tom calls the team for a victory celebration, but it is a muted affair.

After taking their extra holidays, Kayleigh and Negash both accept offers from big consulting companies, leaving the company with no one to support large chunks of functionalities on their newly implemented platform.

Problem

The Hero anti-pattern generally purports to fix an urgent delivery problem that has occurred either in a project context, as in our example, or during normal operations. When it occurs in normal operational mode, this is often in a context where firefighting issues with the system have become a run-of-the-mill occurrence.

Usually, the problem occurs in a context characterized by some of the following factors:

- There are limited resources to carry out the work needed to fix the urgent problem and there are good reasons why new resources cannot be brought in at this time.

- The project has a tight schedule that is perceived to be set in stone or the issue is live, critical, and affecting important business users adversely in ways that cause a lot of noise.

- There is knowledge about the problem concentrated in a small number of heads, that is to say, a few people, such as Kayleigh and Negash, who volunteered to take on the role, or frequently a lead developer who is the only one with the technical knowledge to fix the issue at the given time.

- The situation is considered somehow special: either this is a new project and there isn't a precedent, or the issue is considered so unique that you can't really plan for it.

- The crisis element is often quite visible in situations that foster the Hero anti-pattern. Sometimes, important parts of the company's future success or even survival are brought into play.

These factors can all make the problem seem more important to fix in a limited time scale and make the Hero option seem attractive.

Proposed solution

The Hero anti-pattern proposes to solve the problem described in the preceding section by allowing an individual or a small group to take too much responsibility for resolving it effectively by working as much as is required, even at some cost to themselves, to get things done.

This can be attractive both to management and to the people involved for a variety of reasons:

- The effort does tend to produce some results in the short term, giving a sense of momentum and success.

- Everyone, or at least nearly everyone, wants to be a hero and be singled out for praise and rewards. To some people, that is worth the inconvenience of the additional effort.

- It is always possible to imagine that the current situation is somehow unique and not reflective of a deeper problem with process or culture within the organization, thereby justifying what is done as exceptional.

- Even if we acknowledge that there are underlying issues, often these can be put out of mind as something to be dealt with later. Of course, in organizations that rely on the Hero anti-pattern, later never comes.

There are several common variants of the Hero anti-pattern that are worth mentioning:

- Superman, a variant where someone, usually a senior technical person, is glorified and held up as the only person who can fix serious issues with a given system. Often, this myth becomes self-perpetuating.

- Rookies, the variant seen in the example, where junior team members take on extra responsibilities in an effort to step up to the challenge that is being presented to them.

- No Time for Knowledge Transfer, a situation where heroics are required by a seemingly never-ending time crunch that would make it possible for the hero or heroes to transfer required knowledge to others.

While this anti-pattern is clearly seductive, and many of us have fallen prey to it several times over the course of our careers, it almost invariably has negative long-term consequences, which we'll explore next.

Results

While the Hero anti-pattern tends to give good short-term results, which is a major source of its enduring appeal, there is a long list of negative results that tend to accumulate over time in organizations that rely on this anti-pattern to get things done.

Some of the most common negative results include the following:

- The creation of a single point of failure that increases risks to an organization substantially, should the Hero fall under the proverbial bus, and gives the Hero a lot of leverage in negotiations with the organization.

- The Hero, over time, will start to feel the pressure, as Kayleigh and Negash did in our example, but will have very limited options to change the situation. This situation is highly conducive to burnout, which brings with it all the problems of the first point as well as the risk of the Hero making serious errors due to the strain.

- Heroes don't scale. That is to say, the organization won't be able to deploy projects at a bandwidth that is wider than what the Hero can accommodate. This can be seriously limiting to new initiatives in some cases.

- Heroes aren't replicable. You can't easily replicate the Hero or their special powers and therefore you have limited options for creating a predictable and repeatable process.

- Heroes can accumulate serious technical debt, which may often go unmanaged, because they must do things quickly, under pressure, and without real supervision. This can lead to major maintenance issues in the long term.

- There is low transparency into the process by which Heroes get things done, leading to a lack of predictability and manageability.

- Heroes don't have time to explain how things were implemented, so there is often poor or entirely missing documentation.

- The rest of the team may feel disempowered, overlooked, and demotivated as all the attention goes to the Heroes, with little opportunity for others to make contributions in a non-heroic way.

You don't necessarily see all these negative outcomes in all instances of this anti-pattern, and this list unfortunately isn't exhaustive either. But hopefully, this is enough to make you think twice about applying this anti-pattern and look at better options, which we'll explore next.

Better solutions

The fundamental problem with the Hero anti-pattern is that you are relying on specific individuals, with often hidden knowledge, working hard – usually too hard – to get things done rather than on repeatable, transparent, and manageable processes that will allow you to continue to deliver, even as the context and the people involved change.

The primary way to get away from the Hero anti-pattern is therefore to work on your processes and spread skills and knowledge systematically across the team. In our example, there were potential issues with scope management, with the initial discovery work, with governance and its understanding of the real issues on the ground, and with the way the project had been structured to go live with a big bang rather than in small increments.

What specific interventions will provide the most leverage will vary a lot between organizations, but some good places to look include the following:

- Moving towards a DevOps culture with smaller incremental releases that have lower risk profiles

- Having multi-functional teams with frequent direct collaboration and peer review to spread knowledge around

- Encouraging and rewarding leads and specialists more for mentoring and bringing up juniors rather than for putting out the latest fire

- Incorporating better risk management and governance in projects to have the right contingencies in place when things go wrong, as they inevitably will

- Challenging the cultural norms that put primacy on delivering big dramatic wins against the odds, rather than on making steady, undramatic, but repeatable progress on a regular basis

- Emphasize roles and processes, not individuals when planning, building, and operating systems, especially when communicating with the wider stakeholder community

- Make the costs of the Hero anti-pattern visible by capturing the technical debt, the risk, and the missed opportunity to be able to replicate efforts that the organization loses by relying on this pattern

- Ensure that detailed requirements and edge cases are planned for when beginning the project, which reduces the probability that you will need a hero

In truth, it is not always possible to completely avoid the Hero anti-pattern. Sometimes, things are on fire and there is only one person around who can fix it. What we need to recognize is that this is not a good situation, but an anti-pattern that we need to work hard to fix so that it doesn't recur. The more you do this, the less you'll have to rely on heroes and the fewer fires you'll have to put out.

Having covered our first example of a real anti-pattern, we will go on to analyze it a little more deeply to see how we can maximize our learning from it.

Analyzing the example

The Hero anti-pattern is a classic and most seasoned IT professionals will have encountered it during their careers. However, interesting as it is, in this book, we are also looking to pull out the larger patterns, we can learn from our examples to hone our architecture skills.

Throughout this book, we will do this by having a section towards the end of a chapter that extracts key learning points for you to take on your future architecture journey. We do this both with a mind to real-life practice, but we also list learning points specifically for those of you who are on the track towards the CTA exam.

Considering the Hero anti-pattern, a few learning points you might extract for real-life practice are as follows:

- When you are faced with a crisis that calls for extraordinary effort on the part of some or all of the team, take the time to step back and consider the process failures that led to this situation. Capture this for future use.

- Relying on a small number of extremely skilled individuals can be dangerous in the long run, even if it's useful right now.

- The pressure you might feel towards going above and beyond may reflect a culture that doesn't have its priorities right from a technical point of view. You may want to challenge that if possible.

- Go out of your way to empower and bring up junior staff to avoid being in the position where you have to be the hero.

- Be diligent about advocating for good governance both at the project and technical levels as well as capturing and remedying the technical debt that accumulates from "special" situations.

Looking at the CTA review board, you can note the following lessons:

- Be careful about suggesting big bang delivery approaches. They can be the right choice, but frequently they can lead to the issues highlighted in the example. Prefer using agile, incremental approaches unless there is a specific reason not to.

- Ensure that you do include the necessary governance functions, including **Project Management Office (PMO)**, steering committee, design authority, and maybe a change advisory board. In this example, much could have been avoided if the latter two had been in place.

- Be explicit about risks and risk management. Include risks upfront and be ready to talk about how to manage and mitigate them.

While we will be able to directly pull out many learning points, we also encourage you to go further with this method and see how much more you can get out of them. Learning from anti-patterns is a continuous and very rewarding activity for aspiring architects.

We have now achieved a foundational understanding of what anti-patterns are and how they can help us achieve greater mastery of Salesforce architecture. It only remains to summarize our progress before we dive into the deep end by looking at anti-patterns in the system architecture domain.

Summary

Phew, that was a lot of background. Thank you for sticking with it. You are now in a position to move forward with the book having understood the key facts about what anti-patterns are and how you can learn from them.

A few things to remember as you go into the next chapters are as follows:

- It is important not to simply think about anti-patterns as bad practice. Bad practice is obvious, but anti-patterns are nefarious. They masquerade as good solutions and can be persuasive in certain situations, even to experienced professionals. That's also what makes them so fun to study.

- While we will be presenting a lot of individual anti-patterns in this book, it is important to draw out the parallels and meta-patterns that can be gleaned by comparing and contrasting them. We will do some of that work for you in the analysis sections that can be found throughout the book. You should also try to do this activity for yourself.

- While we are focusing on a Salesforce context, many of the patterns you will learn about are applicable to other platforms as well. Some are even classics that will be known by a great number of grizzled architects.

With that out of the way, we are now ready to look in detail at our first architecture domain: systems architecture.

2

How Not to Mess Up Your System Architecture

This chapter will start with an explanation of how you mess up your system landscape by not retaining a disciplined approach to implementation and governance. We will then go through how coupling can become so tight that you create systems too fragile to use. Finally, we will look at some anti-patterns related to how you can structure orgs within an organization that uses Salesforce into multiple geographies and business units.

In this chapter, we're going to cover the following main topics:

- How the Stovepipe anti-pattern can leave us with systems that can only work in isolation and what you can do to avoid building stovepipes

- What a Big Ball of Mud is, why a system can deteriorate into a state that fits this description, and how you can prevent it from happening to your system

- How intense coupling makes systems fragile and potentially unusable, and how to draw clearer system boundaries that avoid this issue

- What unfettered org creation can do to your enterprise architecture and how to better manage your Salesforce environments

After completing this chapter, you will have a good grasp of some of the main maladies that can afflict a Salesforce system architecture. You will also learn about the key things to look out for in your architecture practice to avoid going down a path that will lead you to these anti-patterns or suggesting a solution prone to these kinds of issues when sitting for the CTA Review Board.

Muddling up the systems landscape

The easiest way to muddle up your systems landscape, as we shall see, is to go ahead with implementation in a local, unstructured, and badly governed way. While there are many attractions to small local projects, they very easily deteriorate into anti-patterns that have serious negative consequences for your overall enterprise architecture. We will start by looking at the classic Stovepipe anti-pattern, which is a common outgrowth of such projects, and then look at its organizational cousin, *Stovepipe Enterprise*.

Stovepipe

A stovepipe is a system that is built with no attention to standards or common abstractions, leading to a system that may work but is hard to maintain, extend, or interoperate with.

An example

John is the CRM manager at DreamCo, a provider of bespoke travel accessories. The company has decided to invest in a small implementation of Salesforce Sales Cloud, replacing an old Siebel system that's been in operation for more than a decade. While initially fearful, John has come to be quite excited about the project, as it promises to fix a number of thorny issues that they've been unable to address with the old CRM.

DreamCo hires a small local Salesforce consultancy to do the implementation. Initially, it is a great success, the sales teams love the new tool, and many of the features requested by John are readily implemented. However, after a while, progress seems to slow and the price of changes goes up. DreamCo's CIO makes the assessment that their business requirements are now too complex for the small local consultancy to manage and hire a leading Salesforce Summit partner to take over.

At the same time, DreamCo's head of customer service decides to commission a third Salesforce partner to implement Salesforce Service Cloud for the company's call center. John has been learning a lot about Salesforce during the initial period and is starting to get worried that there are no common conventions, standards, methodologies, or tools across the different partners or implementations. The sales department and the customer service department also seem to use very different data models to represent fundamentally the same things.

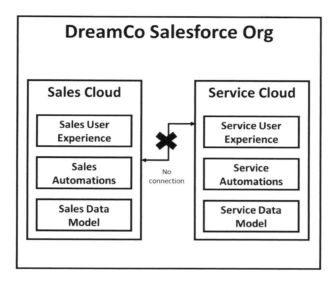

Figure 2.1 – DreamCo's org after the initial implementations

John raises these points to the CIO and asks for a budget to hire an architect and to do some refactoring on the existing systems to bring them more in line. He is told that while his idea is good, it isn't affordable right now, but he should put in a budget request for next year's budget.

At this time, DreamCo purchases a smaller company that sells travel accessories via vending machines in airports. They reportedly have a very strong Salesforce implementation, much more advanced than DreamCo's, including sales, service, and field service modules. John is given the task of finding a way to consolidate the two Salesforce orgs into one without requiring the two organizations to fundamentally change their processes.

John engages with the Summit partner to explore options for the consolidation. They come back with a proposal that meets the basic requirement, but at a cost that is much higher than expected. The partner explains that the excessive technical complexity in the DreamCo org makes it very difficult to integrate with the new org. Furthermore, they advise against going down the consolidation route and instead advise DreamCo to move everyone to the org from the company that has been recently acquired and change the processes to make this work without changing the technology.

After some internal discussion, DreamCo decides to go ahead with the consolidation anyway. Problems start appearing almost right away:

- First, it proves very difficult for the different vendors that need to be involved to collaborate effectively, leading to a situation where the lead partner is effectively required to reverse-engineer a number of features in order to understand them.

- Second, the implementation progress is very slow and John realistically can see no way for the project to complete on time.

- Third, the error rate is very high and there are many recurring errors on each test cycle. All of this is leading toward a project that will be significantly over budget, behind schedule, and below expectation on quality.

John starts digging into the detail, and from the various technical people involved in the project, he learns a number of disturbing facts. First, basic things such as naming conventions are completely different, not only between the DreamCo and the NewCo org but also within the DreamCo org; at least three completely different sets of conventions exist. In addition, features are implemented using completely different methodologies and toolsets, and sometimes the same feature is reimplemented in different ways in different parts of the system.

There are also a number of custom fields and objects that exist in subtly different duplicated variants in different parts of the system. Finally, a number of third-party tools have been used to provide functionality. However, these tools and their functions were never properly documented and no one in the organization knows how to use them after the change of vendors. Adding this to the inherent complexity involved in finding a common language between the DreamCo and the NewCo orgs, most of the technical teams are starting to throw their hands up in despair.

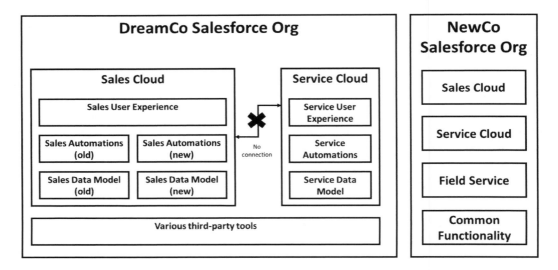

Figure 2.2 – The DreamCo consolidation scenario

John reports this back to senior management and the situation escalates into a major crisis. Eventually, after much wrangling, DreamCo gives up on consolidating the two orgs and decides to leave them in place separately instead for the time being, with data consolidated elsewhere for reporting.

The problem

How do you implement an IT system in an organization where departments are siloed, power is distributed into individual fiefdoms, technical teams work independently of each other, and there is no strong central authority on architecture or technical standards? The answer, in general, is the *stovepipe anti-pattern*. Given the prevalence of these organizational characteristics, stovepipe is one of the most common anti-patterns you are likely to encounter as an architect.

Let's not disregard how hard it is to get around some of these issues. Changing organizational structures or cultures can require years of transformation, even with senior management support, and even then, many unfortunate practices may still linger.

So, when you are an ambitious manager with the need for a new IT system in the kind of organization described above, it is very tempting to simply go ahead within your own little kingdom and implement something, working with people that you personally trust, in a way that works for you, without much consideration for the rest of the business. Without strong corporate IT governance and enterprise architecture support, there is little most IT departments can do about this.

The stovepipe anti-pattern then does provide a real answer to a real problem, as we will discuss in the next section. However, it is an answer that reliably leads to unfortunate results.

The proposed solution

Fundamentally, a stovepipe proposes to solve the coordination problems inherent in many organizations by building a solution in splendid isolation, not taking into account any wider concerns or requirements, using whatever tooling and standards the implementing team prefers. That way, you can simply go ahead while short-circuiting corporate bureaucracy in the process.

This is an attractive solution in a number of ways:

- You do not have to engage in cross-silo collaboration or resolve thorny internal political issues
- Your technical teams often love it because they can use whatever tools they prefer to get the job done
- It tends to work very well in the short term, quickly delivering on requirements and generating local value, often at a very reasonable price point
- For organizations without strong central IT leadership, it can be the default way to operate, and it may simply become "the way things get done"

If we were living in a simpler world, where organizations could compartmentalize their operations between discreet groups that didn't have to collaborate much to get things done, and consequently, systems didn't have to support cross-cutting workflows or cross-system integrations, then a stovepipe would actually be a perfectly reasonable approach to software development.

However, in practice, most organizations do need most of their systems to work across a wide range of departments and use cases, which is when we start to get into trouble, as we'll see in the next section.

The result

As previously pointed out, and as we saw in our example, a stovepipe often initially works well. For a point solution used by a single team, there isn't any inherent downside to building in this local way. As we saw, the issues start to accumulate when we have multiple players on the same underlying platform, for example, the Sales and Service organizations we mentioned, when we try to extend the system to use cases it wasn't designed for, and when we need it to play well with other external systems.

On Salesforce, it is normal to have many different modules in simultaneous operation in the same org that leverage a common data model, user interface, and technical configuration. Unfortunately, this makes it particularly easy to end up with stovepipe-type problems if you do not implement these modules consistently.

Over time, the indicators of a stovepipe anti-pattern tend to be the following:

- An increasing difficulty in understanding the code base, especially for new parties working with the system
- Inconsistent architectural design and implementation patterns in different areas of the system
- A diminishing user experience and user value due to the increasing inconsistency and inflexibility of the system
- Great difficulty whenever new requirements have to be implemented
- The system is hard to integrate with other systems in the landscape
- The system is hard to incorporate into global processes, for example, a consolidated DevOps pipeline
- Increasing error rates, both during development and in production
- A higher and higher cost of change due to all these factors

The fundamental reason a stovepipe tends to deteriorate in this way is due to a lack of common standards, practices, patterns, and tooling. Inconsistency increases the cognitive load on the technical team, making everything harder and more error-prone, as well as raising the learning curve across the board. The original team might have understood it, but over time, this understanding will be lost, and the result tends to be more inconsistent, rather than a concerted effort being made to refactor it into a more comprehensible state.

You can profitably compare a team building a stovepipe to a well-functioning agile team to understand what goes wrong. An agile team may also work in relative isolation with empowered Product Owners calling the shots. However, they will work with standards, practices, patterns, and tools that are accepted and well-understood in the organization, and they will work with stable interfaces for key integrations and common abstractions for crucial system components. That way, coordination happens implicitly via that common baseline and you do not end up with a stovepipe, but rather, a well-adjusted member of the system landscape.

Better solutions

The fact is that many organizations are quite siloed, and it therefore becomes hard to solve the business-level coordination problems that arise when building, implementing, or changing systems. As architects, dealing with these issues should be part of our bread-and-butter activities in order to avoid building stovepipe systems and ensure that our platforms, such as Salesforce, continue to deliver value over the long term.

While some of the more transformative things that can be done organizationally to break down silos and improve collaboration are often beyond our power, there are many things that we can reliably do to improve the situation:

- Define clear architectural patterns and practices that can be used between teams to create common abstractions

- Put in place conventions for how different things are to be implemented, both at the macro level, for example, when to use flows and when to use triggers, and micro level, such as a coding guideline

- Adopt standards for all technical areas, such as reporting and BI or data governance, in order to ensure consistency

- Have strong guidance for creating stable interfaces for cross-system integration, as well as integration patterns for different use cases

- Put in place a common methodology for implementation across Salesforce projects to ensure consistency

- Adopt consistent tooling for all elements of the development life cycle to enable cross-team and cross-system understanding

- Enforce these standards and practices vigorously

We are in a fortunate position as Salesforce architects in that much of this work can be taken from good practices already in existence, either established by Salesforce themselves or the wider Salesforce community. You can find many good resources on the Salesforce Architects website, and Salesforce has also recently introduced the **Salesforce Operating, Governance, and Architecture (SOGAF)** framework to help us understand the best practices for Salesforce governance:

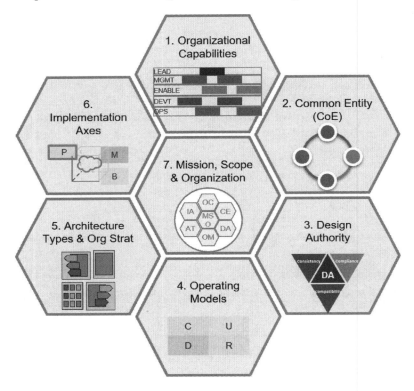

Figure 2.3 – SOGAF framework elements

However, we always have the responsibility to adopt, adapt, and implement it within our own organizations ourselves. This also includes adding the business-specific standards and practices that are unique to our situation and finding ways of communicating the standards and practices in a way that resonates across our organization.

It should be noted that sometimes standards should be broken. There are cases where you need different tools, methods, or patterns to get the job done, but you should have a standard to deviate from if you want to avoid ending up building stovepipes.

A note on Stovepipe Enterprise

The material we have discussed on this pattern so far has focused primarily on the system level. However, it will not have escaped a more perceptive reader that many of the issues that appear on the system level are related to organizational issues, particularly the tendency for some organizations to work in silos and be unproductively political.

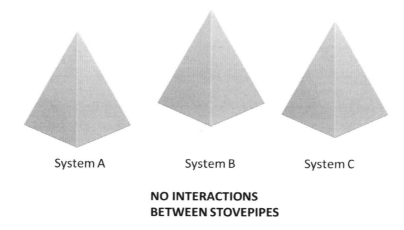

**NO INTERACTIONS
BETWEEN STOVEPIPES**

Figure 2.4 – A landscape of stovepipes making up a stovepipe enterprise

As a result, there's an organizational-level version of the stovepipe anti-pattern called Stovepipe Enterprise, which focuses on this tendency of organizations to produce stovepipe systems due to their structural problems. While we can readily acknowledge this anti-pattern, as Salesforce architects, our remit does not usually extend to this level of problem, and we have therefore mostly focused on the system level in our discussion.

A Big Ball of Mud

> *A Big Ball of Mud is a system that has lost all internal structure and coherence and can only be partially understood by its original creator(s) and not at all by anyone else.*

An example

DreamCo has put adding more functionality to their Salesforce implementation on hold for a few months. During this time, John has been working on a plan to refactor key parts of the system to make it more maintainable. He's been consulting a lot of technical people from the different teams that have been involved since day one and he finally thinks he has found a way forward.

However, shortly before John has a meeting to pitch his ideas to the CIO, things change rapidly on the ground. DreamCo has recently hired Ricky, an experienced architect from one of the big consultancies, to help figure out how to integrate the DreamCo and NewCo orgs. While he has generally been supportive of John's effort to get refactoring started, it clearly hasn't been at the top of his agenda.

Instead, he proposes to focus DreamCo's efforts on the Salesforce side into an integration project to combine the two orgs. He proposes to do much of the technical work himself, using a third-party tool that he has previously used on other projects. The integration will be point-to-point, but it will reliably ferry the data needed back and forth between the two environments, and end the complex manual processes that the business has had to use to bridge the gap in the interim.

Given the pressure on the business, the CIO decides to go ahead with Ricky's plan, and he implements the solution over a two-month period more or less single-handedly. John is told that his refactoring project will get the go-ahead after the integration is complete. However, once it's done, the CIO gives the go-ahead to a new set of feature upgrades on the existing platform for both the Sales and Service teams. John is told that the business can't wait for any new features and that instead, he will need to lead the development of a new logistics app that the business wants to build in a separate Salesforce org, with Ricky acting as the technical lead.

The new app is built quickly in the new environment but John remains concerned that it is being built with very little structure or discipline. The business seems to love what they're seeing, so John relents and lets things go ahead, supporting where he can. While the app was meant to be an experimental prototype, the business decides they want to put it into production as is. The upgrade to the main org takes a long time to get done, but the day for the production deployment finally approaches.

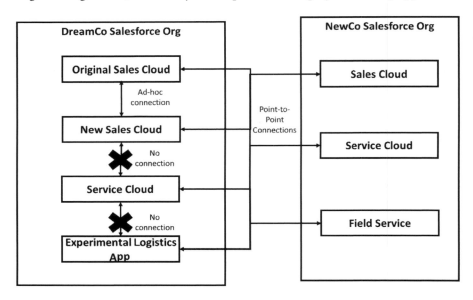

Figure 2.5 – The DreamCo Big Ball of Mud architecture

DreamCo will deploy the new upgrades as well as the new logistics app into the production org in a single deployment over a weekend. All hands are on deck and there is a positive buzz around the release, as many of these features, as well as the new app, are avidly anticipated. The last weeks are slightly marred by Ricky handing in his notice, as he has decided to take an offer from another consultancy. However, he promises to document and hand over everything before he leaves, so no one is overly concerned.

On the weekend it is going live, John is on call and avidly awaiting the results. The initial deployment runs into some issues and the full deployment doesn't actually make it into production before Sunday afternoon. The test team starts their smoke test and it is obvious that there are major problems with the release. Major functional areas don't seem to be working, the integration between the DreamCo and the NewCo org starts experiencing errors, and many test scripts that were working in the main org or the logistics org fail completely. Questions are raised about the quality of UAT testing but the fact is that the release has failed.

The team works frantically overnight to get the system back to a reasonable state before the business starts using it in the morning. Communications go out stating that the release had to be pulled back. DreamCo's board calls the CIO for a consultation on what went wrong. However, no one can work it out, and for both the logistics app and the DreamCo to NewCo integration, it seems to be impossible to fix any issues now that Ricky has gone, despite knowledge transfer sessions having taken place.

After a week of finger-pointing back and forth, the CIO is fired and a replacement comes in. He commissions a detailed technical audit of the current system from a consultancy that he personally trusts. After consultation with John and many other DreamCo stakeholders, they conclude that the architecture and code quality on many components is so weak and the structure so incomprehensible that the only option is to rebuild significant parts of the system.

The problem

A Big Ball of Mud is what happens when all internal structure within a system collapses and what you are left with is a big ball of undifferentiated mud that is impossible to understand or change. In contrast to a stovepipe, which can work quite well within its own limited sphere, a Big Ball of Mud is effectively a throwaway system. You might be able to keep it running with enough firefighting, but you'll never make it work well or significantly change it. It is a response to a system that has such great pressure to deliver functionality in several areas, that going along with any idea that seems to deliver the functionality in question seems to be a good idea.

It happens usually either as a result of ignorance or desperation, as no one intentionally sets out to create a big mess. You do, however, frequently get Big Balls of Mud from systems that have been created due to one person or a couple of people working independently without supervision, clear documentation, or good decision-making processes, as with Ricky in our example.

You could say that a Big Ball of Mud shares the Nike approach to implementation, "*Just Do It.*" While this may be a good principle in athletics, it rarely works out well in enterprise IT.

The proposed solution

The solution proposed by a Big Ball of Mud, in general, is to put your trust in some team or person to just get something done with no regard for the consequences. It is often attractive in pressured situations because it gives you a seemingly good way out of your predicament without having to pay the costs of disciplined development or implementation.

Big Balls of Mud often evolve from systems such as Stovepipes, when all discipline and control are lost. A stovepipe, if it is true to its own internal structure, can work well on its own for a long period of time, but once you give up on this internal discipline, it quickly devolves into a Big Ball of Mud.

Big Balls of Mud are also often created from experimental or prototype systems that are elevated to production status, as with the logistics app in our earlier example. The results of a system reaching the Big Ball of Mud stage are usually catastrophic, as we'll discuss in the following section.

The results

A Big Ball of Mud is an end state for a system. Once the system reaches a state of total internal disorganization, the only way to keep it running is to have the one or two people who still partially understand how it works continuously firefighting to keep it going. You will neither be able to make changes that are anything other than trivial nor will it be realistic to refactor the system into a reasonable state. It would be cheaper to rebuild the key modules, which is what tends to eventually happen with these kinds of systems.

As noted in the introduction, some people like to be heroes, and also like the job security that comes from being indispensable, so the period during which a Big Ball of Mud can remain operational is surprisingly long in some cases.

The fundamental solution to the Big Ball of Mud scenario is technical discipline in various forms, which we'll discuss next.

Better solutions

In many ways, the better solution to the Big Ball of Mud anti-pattern is similar to those we listed for the stovepipe. If you have good technical standards and practices in place and they are followed in practice, then you will not end up with a Big Ball of Mud.

More fundamentally, though, the Big Ball of Mud scenario reveals a profound lack of technical discipline and respect for craftsmanship within the executing organization. If your technical culture does not value good practice, architecture, well-structured code, and abstractions, but instead values cowboys just getting something up and running, no matter how quick and dirty, then you will be prone to end up with Big Balls of Mud.

To be sure, there are situations where quick and dirty is good enough. If you're writing code for an ephemeral marketing campaign, a research project, or a throwaway prototype, then you don't have to care so much about whether the system you create can evolve. However, for most of us, most of the time, this is not the case.

Too much coupling

Designing systems with low coupling and high coherence is one of the foundational aims of software architects of any stripe. Coupling, however, can be difficult to avoid and in many cases, a level of coupling can be justified as a trade-off with other concerns. In this section, however, we will see how intense coupling can become an anti-pattern that seriously affects your system architecture.

Intense coupling

Intense coupling is an anti-pattern where one or more systems in the system landscape fails to maintain clear boundaries with other coupled systems, leading to a fragile and unmaintainable state.

An example

BigCo has a mid-size Sales Cloud implementation that they use for managing their opportunity pipeline. However, all financial processes, quoting, and order management is done in their main SAP system, which has served as the source of truth for the business for a number of years.

The sales department loves their Salesforce system and would like to carry out the entire ordering and fulfilment process through Salesforce, leaving the SAP system to the purely financial processes. The finance and supply chain teams think this idea is not only misguided, but risks compromising the strong grip BigCo has had on its data for years.

After some internal political battles, the CFO and VP of Sales reach a compromise. The order and fulfilment process will stay in SAP, along with the financial processes, but quoting will move end-to-end to Salesforce using Salesforce CPQ. That way, the sales team will rarely need to go into SAP and can stay primarily in the Salesforce interface that they love, but the other teams still keep control of all master data. Anitha, a Salesforce architect, is tasked with making this compromise into reality.

She quickly discovers some major issues with this approach:

- First, all products and prices are kept directly in SAP and there is no appetite for moving this to Salesforce; therefore, it will need to be accessed from SAP as part of the quoting process and only stub data can be replicated to Salesforce.

- Second, a number of business logic checks happen for quotes during the business process to check that they fall within acceptable corporate parameters. Anitha looks into moving these checks to Salesforce as part of the implementation. While it is possible for many, some of these checks require access to data in SAP's financial module and can't be done on Salesforce. These will need to be accessed via an integration to SAP too.

- Third, a number of additional services need to be called as part of the quoting process to get current product availability and possible delivery dates for inclusion on the quote. These will have to be called via SAP, as they are already exposed via webservices on this platform, and BigCo does not have the integration resources to make a direct connection to Salesforce or to connect via other middleware.

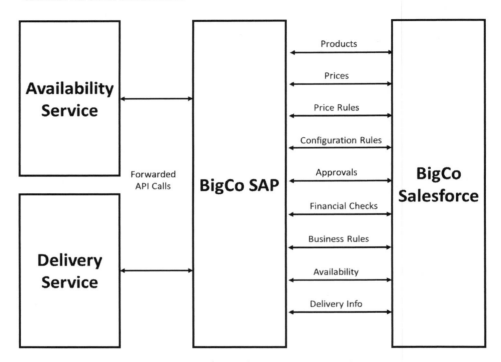

Figure 2.6 – The BigCo integration scenario

Anitha sounds the alarm and says that the degree to which Salesforce depends on SAP makes her doubt that the new system will perform to the high expectations of the sales team. She recommends looking into a different approach where there is a cleaner division between what is on SAP and what is on Salesforce. However, the Finance and Supply Chain teams rule out any process changes as part of the implementation and therefore she has to go ahead despite her doubts.

The initial workshops with users go well and the functional requirements of the sales team seem to be a good fit for what Salesforce has to offer. However, Anitha is still concerned that the final product will underperform due to the coupling to SAP.

During the UAT testing of the solution, some concerns are raised about the performance and responsiveness of the user interface, and there are also complaints that testing had to be interrupted several times due to maintenance or outages on SAP.

These concerns are not enough to hold back the go-live, however, as the team expects a boost in performance from moving to the production environment, and the basic functional aspects of the solution are acceptable.

Unfortunately, the problems are exacerbated and not alleviated by the move to production. Performance decreases significantly and sales users frequently have to wait for minutes to see a response from SAP. In addition, there are numerous periods during the day when SAP runs large scheduled jobs that stop sales users from doing anything.

The team works frantically to try to improve the situation. However, after a couple of weeks, the team has to throw in the towel and the sales team goes back to producing their quotes in SAP.

The problem

Intense coupling happens when the boundaries between systems or modules are blurred to such an extent that one depends entirely on the other for its operation. In general, as architects, we strive to reduce coupling while maintaining coherence. However, coupling – even tight coupling – can be a necessary trade-off with other requirements in some situations.

Intense coupling, however, is the most extreme version of this trade-off. At the system level, it happens when system boundaries are not respected, and you try to design a solution that incorporates and replicates significant parts of another system, using the other system as a synchronous backend.

The same pattern can repeat at the module level, where you have one module replicating all the functionality of another in a different context, calling intensely on functionality from the original module to do so.

Intense coupling is often done for good reason. There are usually real problems with the functionality of legacy systems or modules that are proving hard to address and that would seemingly be much simpler to solve in a different system or module context.

As we'll see in the following section, the proposal that intense coupling makes to address such issues can be very compelling, which is what makes it a classic anti-pattern.

Proposed solutions

Intense coupling is a proposition that promises that you can have your cake and eat it too. By using APIs or SDKs, or using some other similar mechanism, you can get all the functionality and business logic that you are used to. Additionally, you can have it work within a new user experience that will address your changing requirements, and you won't have to go through the pain of introducing a new system or making substantial changes to your legacy ones. As with all cake-related propositions of this kind, you should be quite skeptical about the truth of these surface claims.

Salesforce is particularly prone to this anti-pattern because it has a user interface that many users love and the business is used to things being fairly easy to implement on the platform. It is therefore common for a request to be made for parts of other systems to be incorporated into the Salesforce platform.

This can be done successfully if you are careful about the boundaries, are open to making the necessary process changes, and have a strong integration capability in place. However, it is also quite easy to end up in an intensely coupled scenario.

The results

Intense coupling tends to result in an end-to-end user experience that is characterized by fragility, instability, and low performance. This happens for the fairly obvious reason that an intensely coupled system is for all intents and purposes a single-user-facing system encompassing two underlying technical systems. It is a distributed system that has not been built with the awareness that it is a distributed system.

The more you need to rely on the other system, the more frequently you need to call out and access its functionality. This means you have an issue whenever either system has an issue in any of the areas that are part of the solution.

You also get the brittleness that comes from any changes to relevant functionality on either side of the system being likely to result in required changes to your intensely coupled system. This means that you will likely see more errors and issues over time than you'd expect.

In addition, the cumulative wait for the functionality going back and forth between the two sides of the intensely coupled system leads to reduced performance, sometimes to the extent that the system becomes unusable.

On the module level, the consequences tend to be more about reduced maintainability, lower flexibility, and higher cost of change, but performance issues will also occasionally creep in.

Better solutions

While the problems that lead to intense coupling are often legitimate, there are many things you as an architect can do to avoid the situation resulting in an anti-pattern. The following list provides a starting point:

- Keep a keen eye on system and module boundaries, and ensure that if they shift, the cut is made at a maintainable point.

- When designing a cross-boundary process, be very clear on system responsibilities and the integration architecture that will support those processes.

- Adapt processes so that they work seamlessly with the revised system boundaries. Don't try to compensate with extra technical work if the processes don't fit.

- Avoid redundant functionality in multiple systems. Be clear on where an engagement with a given set of functionalities is done.

- If what you are building is in fact a distributed system, be mindful of that fact and use low-coupling integration patterns, such as event-based integration, to achieve your goals. Resist calls for large amounts of synchronous integration.

Having now discussed a number of patterns that are applicable to Salesforce, as well as many other technologies, we will now move on to our first unique Salesforce anti-pattern, Ungoverned Org Proliferation.

Org complications

In the Salesforce world, you don't have to manage your underlying infrastructure, which frees you from a good number of potential temptations that can lead to anti-patterns. However, the way that you structure environments with different orgs in the Salesforce world is subject to a number of anti-patterns in its own right.

Ungoverned Org Proliferation

> *Ungoverned Org Proliferation is a Salesforce-specific anti-pattern due to a lack of defined org strategy, which leaves you with an ever-increasing number of unaligned orgs, eventually becoming architecturally unmanageable.*

An example

Miranda has been hired as BigCo's new CRM Migration Manager. The company has had a business unit approach to IT and does not have any centralized CRM capabilities at this point. Instead, three units use Salesforce mainly for opportunity management, and there are at least 15 other systems in use from a variety of vendors, as well as in-house developed systems in play across departments and geographies.

Miranda has been tasked with consolidating this landscape, using Salesforce as the primary platform. There is a general aim to consolidate systems and standardize processes, but there are few central resources to drive this transformation.

Miranda plans a strategy to consolidate around the three existing Salesforce orgs. She has previously been through org consolidation projects in Salesforce and doesn't think there is enough value to go through that pain in this case.

She will therefore create three variants of a core Salesforce implementation, dispersed across three geographies, and map the other CRM systems to whichever of these three is the best fit. She will implement reporting processes across these three orgs using the corporate data warehouse that already imports Salesforce data from two of the orgs.

However, as she starts to plan for migrations, she faces massive pushback from business users on her plans. While most teams are quite willing to move to Salesforce, users in France and China, two of BigCo's largest markets, demand their own unique and segregated environments.

According to the country leads, this is a legal requirement and not up for discussion. Miranda escalates the question to the Legal department but is unable to get answer out of them quickly. She therefore has to accept the separate orgs for France and China.

BigCo's largest market is the UK, and the country lead there, once he understands that having a separate environment is a possibility, demands that they are also given a unique Salesforce org that can be customized specifically to their requirements. The UK operation is highly efficient, but also unique, and there is no way it would work with the same processes as the rest of the business, the argument goes.

Once again, Miranda finds herself politically outgunned and has to assent to these demands. However, this leads to a new opening of the floodgates. Product development argue that their process is distinct enough to merit a separate environment, and similar requests from other departments and geographical units follow.

At the end of the day, Miranda will be looking at a dozen different Salesforce orgs, with many having quite distinctive processes implemented. This is still preferable to the fifteen totally different systems in play before Salesforce, but far from the original goals. At least, she finally has a way forward.

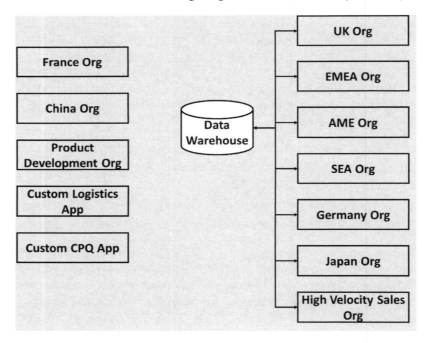

Figure 2.7 – The BigCo org overview

Now, a long-awaited report comes in from a leading management consultancy on how to optimize BigCo's global sales process. This promises major global efficiency in sales and sales operations by moving to a globally standardized process for all field sales. It is implicitly assumed that this global process will be implemented on Salesforce.

Miranda asks around to see whether anyone is willing to change their position on the implementation plans in light of the new objectives. The answer is a resounding no. She decides that enough is enough and hands in her notice the following day.

The problem

Ungoverned Org Proliferation happens in organizations that like Salesforce, but don't like standardizing processes, user interfaces, or other similar requirements, and don't have any strong architectural governance around their Salesforce platform.

The problems that lead to Ungoverned Org Proliferation tend to be found within the following scenarios:

- Different business units or geographies have different processes and can't agree to a compromise that can be implemented

- Different stakeholders have radically different views of how the user experience should be structured and can't agree on a reasonable compromise

- Different stakeholders have radically different views on the data model to be implemented and can't agree on a reasonable compromise

- There are certain critical features which are needed in some business units, but can't be used in others, different integration backends, for example

- Different parts of the business are working with different Salesforce partners that are pushing them in different directions

- There are perceived or real security differences between different parts of the business that strongly impact the Salesforce implementation

- There are perceived or real legal compliance regime differences between different parts of the business that strongly impact the Salesforce implementation

> **Note**
>
> It's worth noting that in the old days, Salesforce actively encouraged organizations to try out the software in a number of different places, the so-called *"seed and grow"* strategy, which worked very well for many years. In large organizations with a long history with Salesforce, you can sometimes still see this legacy living on within rather unstructured org landscapes.

The proposed solution

The proposed solution to the problems leading to Ungoverned Org Proliferation is to give everyone who wants it their own Salesforce org and let them get on with it. This is attractive because it reduces coordination issues, alignment problems, and allows easier resolution of thorny compliance issues. It also lets powerful stakeholders get things in their own way.

There are different variants and degrees of this anti-pattern, some which are relatively benign or even beneficial. In our previous example, some of the asks are probably entirely legitimate and should have been part of a systematically evaluated org strategy. Product development processes, for instance, are often configured in a separate org to the one used for Sales and Service, and sometimes there are real compliance headaches that necessitate multiple orgs.

Let's be clear. There's nothing wrong with a multi-org strategy; it can both be the right architectural choice and work well in practice. However, with Ungoverned Org Proliferation, we are talking about a multi-org operation without any strategy or architecture supporting it, and that tends to result in serious negative consequences, as we'll discuss in the following section.

The results

The result of Ungoverned Org Proliferation is a sprawl of orgs that cannot be controlled from the organization's center. How serious a problem that is will depend on the nature of the organizational culture and how much central control it requires.

In general, you will find some or all of these disadvantages present in an ungoverned org landscape:

- Difficulties in implementing processes that cut across business units or geographical divisions, as the Salesforce implementations vary by data model and components
- Difficulty aligning data for reporting, as the data model and the meaning of fields will be locally defined
- Complexity developing reports, even when data is brought together, due to the semantic gap between different uses of data
- Integrations often have to be replicated in several different places and can be hard to control
- Licensing can get expensive, as some users need multiple licenses
- Knowledge of the systems is heavily distributed and getting an overview of any particular aspect can be hard to find, as technical teams also mostly work in a local context
- Instituting any kind of global governance can be near impossible due to a combination of the aforementioned factors
- As org consolidation is hard, once you find yourself in this situation, it can be difficult to undo

This list is, to a large extent, simply a more extreme version of the downsides of a multi-org strategy, which makes sense, of course. As we will cover in the following section, the key takeaway to avoid this anti-pattern is to clearly define your org strategy up front, along with mitigations for the inevitable downsides.

Better solutions

It will come as no surprise at this point to anyone familiar with Salesforce architecture that the most important element for avoiding this anti-pattern is to have a clearly defined org strategy. This org strategy should clearly define when, if ever, it is permissible to spin up a new Salesforce org, as well as provide clear patterns to use for integration and data consolidation between orgs.

There are a number of good resources you can use to learn about org strategy. I recommend you start with the SOGAF framework that can be found on the Salesforce Architects site: `https://architect.salesforce.com/govern/operating-models/sogaf-operating-models`. This is a comprehensive view from the horse's mouth, although it won't cover all the details that may be required.

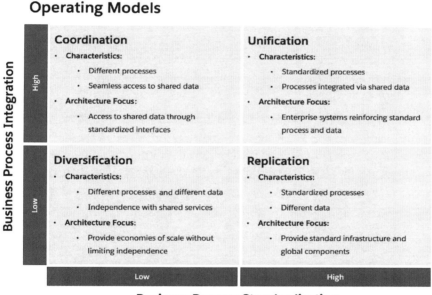

Figure 2.8 – SOGAF models

In addition, in what is becoming a refrain within this book, you should define a common framework for governance, ideally rooted in a **Center of Excellence (CoE)** that has a global oversight of all things Salesforce, and that is followed by all orgs. This framework should also include common standards and practices, and ideally, also a level of common tooling that must be used in every environment.

The opposite of this pattern

It is worth noting that this anti-pattern has an exact opposite, which I like to call a Procrustean Bed, in honor of the Greek mythological figure Procrustes.

This anti-pattern tries to fit all the requirements into a single org across geographies, business functions, and business units. While many organizations do well with a single global org, there are times when multiple orgs are needed to avoid creating a subpar user experience for key stakeholders, make genuinely diverse and business-critical processes work, or solve real legal issues.

That is to say, org strategy is a balancing act, and you can go too far in either direction, turning it into an anti-pattern. You should refer to the SOGAF models mentioned earlier to find the right way forward in your scenario.

Knowing the takeaways

In this section, we will abstract a bit from the specific patterns and instead, try to pull out the wider learning points that you can use in your day-to-day work as a Salesforce architect or when preparing for the CTA Review Board.

When architecting Salesforce solutions, you should be mindful of the following:

- Many organizations are internally siloed and political, and, in these kinds of organizations, the default mode of operation may be to develop Stovepipes or Big Balls of Mud.
- To avoid this, you as a Salesforce architect need to push strongly for countermeasures.
- This will include pushing for strong architecture governance and coordination on Salesforce projects, including establishing relevant governance forums to coordinate activities, and the right technical standards and practices to ensure everyone is building in a consistent way.
- You need to secure enough business support for these initiatives to make them enforceable when things get hectic; this will require careful cultivation and management of relevant stakeholders.
- Design your systems with common abstractions, for instance, by basing different modules on a common package of shared functionality. This will encourage technical consistency between projects.
- Having strong governance about the common elements shared between different Salesforce projects, such as the Hero objects that are used by nearly any Salesforce solution, is necessary.
- These must be used consistently and have clear ownership, or you will end with a mess in your data model and most likely also in your automations.
- Don't have fuzzy boundaries between systems. Make it clear what processing needs to happen where and if the boundaries have to change, make sure it is accompanied by process change to avoid intense-coupling scenarios.

- Favor simpler integration patterns where possible. Favor asynchronous integration patterns over synchronous ones where possible. This helps limit coupling.

- Have a clearly defined org strategy that defines when, if ever, it is appropriate to create a new production org.

- Ensure that relevant stakeholders are consulted before any new org is created, for instance, you can make it subject to approval by a Design Authority or an Architecture Governance board.

- Ensure that common abstractions, standards, practices, and tools are also used in any new orgs.

In preparing for the CTA Review Board, you should be mindful of the following:

- Always include appropriate governance structures to ensure that you have a structured approach to implementation. These may include a Center of Excellence, an **Architecture Governance Forum**, and a **Project Management Office (PMO)**.

- It is also worth mentioning the importance of common patterns, practices, and tools as a way to coordinate implementation activities between teams and ensure maintainability.

- There is often risk associated with stakeholder management if there are multiple different departments or business units involved. As we have seen, bad stakeholder management can be a major contributing factor in selecting an anti-pattern.

- Design a clear system landscape with easy-to-understand roles between the different systems. Avoid having lots of overlap between systems when it comes to core functionality.

- Consider carefully how the different elements in your solution both on and off platform should interact in a way that doesn't introduce a stovepipe such as isolation for some elements. Your solution should present itself as a coherent whole.

- Avoid unnecessary coupling between systems, and avoid especially strong dependencies between systems, where it isn't absolutely critical to the functional experience.

- Favor asynchronous integration patterns that reduce coupling if there isn't a direct need for synchronous communication.

- You should always have an org strategy, you should state it up front, and you should be able to defend it from questioning.

- Be careful not to veer into having either too many orgs that will be extremely difficult to govern effectively or a single org in a scenario that has a strong impetus towards splitting, such as highly variable processes, or definite legal and compliance requirements.

- In any case, be prepared to say how you will mitigate the issues associated with your org strategy, as no scenario is ever clear-cut and there will be trade-offs to consider.

We have now covered the material for this chapter and are ready to proceed. First, however, we will summarize our learning.

Summary

In this chapter, we have seen how you can easily mess up your system architecture in a number of different ways by not carefully attending to architectural matters, good practice, and good governance. You should feel an increased sense of importance about your job as an architect after reading this. Getting things wrong is easy and it is often you who will have to raise the uncomfortable questions that are required to keep the business from veering off a sustainable path, despite the temptations to do so.

We saw that some patterns are common to Salesforce, and many other systems and platforms. These included the following:

- Stovepipes, both at the system and enterprise level
- Big Balls of Mud
- Intensive coupling

However, we also saw that the patterns related to org structure, namely Ungoverned Org Proliferation and its inverse Procrustean Bed, were unique to the Salesforce context. This is something we will come across many times in this book. Salesforce is in many ways a technology platform similar to other technology platforms, but it is also sufficiently unique enough that Salesforce architecture is not so similar to other, more general **SaaS** or **PaaS** architectures in some cases. Learning to distinguish when you are dealing with the unique patterns related to Salesforce and when you need to apply general good practice is a skill particular to the Salesforce architect.

We will now move on to one of the most important topics from the anti-pattern perspective, as errors in this domain can lead to major costs for your organization. Of course, we are referring to security, which will be covered in the next chapter.

How Not to Get Confused about Security

This chapter includes anti-patterns related to securing your Salesforce organization. It will start by reviewing a key anti-pattern around the shared security model that is integral to Salesforce. Then, we will look at anti-patterns that can occur when you mistake things that aren't security for security.

We will continue to look at how not to make a mess of your sharing model and once again finish up with a review of the key points to take away.

In this chapter, we're going to cover the following main topics:

- The *Shared Belongs to Salesforce* anti-pattern and how people get the shared responsibility model wrong

- How the *Compliant Is Secure* anti-pattern lulls you into a false sense of security and what you can do about it

- The *Declarative Is Always Safe* anti-pattern and why you can't rely on declarative features to always be secure

- The *Spaghetti Sharing Model* anti-pattern – why it is deceptively easy to get into an overcomplicated sharing model on Salesforce and how you can prevent it from happening to your organization

After completing this chapter, you will have a good idea about how to avoid common security anti-patterns on Salesforce and what steps you can take to implement better security practices on the platform.

Getting confused about shared responsibility

Almost all SaaS and PaaS platforms use a security model called shared responsibility – that is to say, the vendor takes responsibility for certain parts of the security architecture and others remain the responsibility of the customer. In this section, we will see how misunderstanding this model can lead to issues in the Salesforce case.

Shared Belongs to Salesforce

The Shared Belongs to Salesforce anti-pattern holds that security on the Salesforce platform is always the predominant responsibility of Salesforce.

Example

SmallCo is a provider of specialty lenses for optical instruments. They sell globally and have recently adopted Salesforce Sales Cloud, order management, and B2B commerce to drive electronic commerce directly to business instead of selling exclusively via distributors.

When they did their implementation, the Salesforce platform went through a security review with James, the dedicated security professional that SmallCo has on staff. He evaluated the platform as a whole and was satisfied that the Salesforce platform, including how Salesforce secures its data centers, platform, and web application, met all the standards that SmallCo would expect.

James evaluates the shared responsibility model that Salesforce uses for security and determines that for the initial project, there shouldn't be any need for additional security controls from SmallCo's side. Salesforce will ensure security adequately without additional work being required by SmallCo.

After a period of successful running, SmallCo wants to extend the digital experience and online community adjacent to their web store, and also bring in a much larger number of customers to the web store itself. Mika, a Salesforce product owner at SmallCo, is given the task to run this extension project.

Because of a limited budget, Mika agrees with the implementation partner that they will extend a lot of functionality to anonymous users so that many tasks can be performed without a login. That way, SmallCo can opt for a relatively small login-based license **Stock Keeping Unit (SKU)**.

The system goes live without issue and, as hoped, user numbers go up by more than a factor of 10. Mika and the team celebrate and, after completing the last outstanding minor improvements, start gearing up for the next project.

Just then, Mika receives a security advisory from a Salesforce consultancy that helped with SmallCo's original Salesforce implementation. They point out that a number of new vulnerabilities have been found in Salesforce APIs used within digital experiences. These potentially allow serious exploits if there is a too-open model toward external users.

Mika is initially worried but remembers the conversation he had with James about Salesforce security prior to starting his new project. APIs sound like a core platform feature and, therefore, something Salesforce will take care of. The project is closed, and doing anything new would require finding a new budget, which is difficult. He, therefore, decides to ignore the warning.

Three weeks later, a data dump arrives at an internal SmallCo email address. It contains a data dump with all of SmallCo's proprietary product information and lists of customers and orders. The data dump comes with a ransom demand to be paid in cryptocurrency to a specified address. Otherwise, the data will be made public.

The situation becomes frantic, and external consultants are brought in to help manage the situation. They quickly discover that some very permissive configurations have been made to help the process of making functionality available to external users. These are the likely source of the breach and were also the cause of the security advisory Mika received from the other partner.

SmallCo is very disappointed that Salesforce would leave such a glaring security hole open and raise it with their account manager, who instead points the finger back at the configuration SmallCo has made. SmallCo finally decides that the only thing to do is to pay the ransom and plug the gap.

The external consultants facilitate both of these actions and the external configuration is locked down. SmallCo has to change its license package, but at this point, it has become a small price to pay to avoid a recurrence of recent events.

On the suggestion of its external consultants, SmallCo sets up a process and some software to continuously monitor the security of its Salesforce environment. In addition, Salesforce-related personnel and James from security receive a number of educational sessions on the Salesforce security model. Mika breathes a sigh of relief and gets ready for the next project.

Problem

The *Shared Belongs to Salesforce* anti-pattern is fundamentally about whose job it is to maintain system and platform security. When you're dealing with cloud systems, there is always a level of shared responsibility in play. That means the system or platform provider will maintain some parts of the security and you are responsible for others.

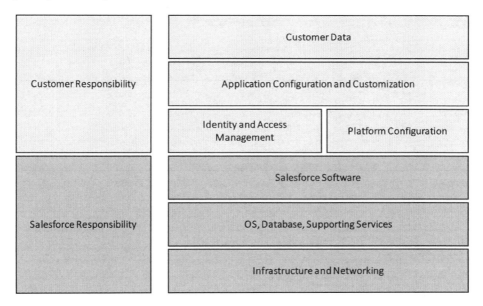

Figure 3.1 – A shared responsibility model

In Salesforce terms, Salesforce maintains infrastructure and platform security and helps you a lot with application layer security. However, when you configure or code something yourself, the responsibility for its security is ultimately on you. While I'm discussing it in the context of Salesforce, it is relevant to all SaaS and PaaS providers, although the specific boundaries defining the shared responsibility will differ.

It is, however, very easy to get confused about this boundary, and that leads to this anti-pattern. The problem that the Shared Belongs to Salesforce anti-pattern seeks to solve is the general security problem – that is to say, *"How can we keep our system secure?"* As we will see with the next system, it proposes to solve the problem by assuming that everything, or at least as much as possible, is the software provider's problem, even when it isn't.

Proposed solution

Shared Belongs to Salesforce proposes to solve the problem of system security by assuming that Salesforce as a world-leading software provider has already thought of all the issues and, therefore, will keep their platform secure. That way, you can safely ignore security as an aspect of your solution and move on with the real work of getting configurations done.

It effectively means that you don't seriously engage with the shared responsibility model, although there are gradations of this. Most organizations, for example, will accept that they have a responsibility for the user permissions that they give the users, who access the system.

However, this might extend to how you configure your sharing model, who you give access to hit APIs or custom-coded classes, or who is allowed to run reports, which makes the situation much murkier. When it gets murky, the adopters of this anti-pattern make the easy choice that they don't have to bother with the complexities because Salesforce will already have thought about it. That, unfortunately, is not and cannot always be true.

This anti-pattern is attractive for a number of reasons:

- You don't have to engage seriously with complex security issues, which means you don't need to hire or develop specialist skills
- It reduces your internal effort when doing work on Salesforce
- It gives you a story to communicate to stakeholders that you are in good hands and don't have to worry about security
- It gives you someone to blame or hold responsible should things go wrong

While you can easily understand why people might be inclined to make their own lives easier by adopting this anti-pattern, the results are not generally optimal.

Results

Humans tend to seek to reduce cognitive load by making simplifications and taking shortcuts. Therefore, the Shared belongs to Salesforce anti-pattern is a naturally occurring phenomenon and it takes active security awareness to counter it.

It is, therefore, not surprising that the first and most serious result of this anti-pattern is a reinforcement of low-security awareness within an organization. If you aren't aware of security issues, it is just a matter of time before something happens. This anti-pattern sets you up for something bad to happen.

Other typical negative results include the following:

- Giving everyone from end users to senior management a false sense of security about their Salesforce system, leading to even more serious fallout when an incident occurs and a lack of understanding that you actually have to do something, rather than Salesforce just fixing it for you.

- Not keeping up with the evolving security landscape on the Salesforce platform. This includes not just ignoring new security advisories as in our example, but also not looking into new security updates or features that would improve your security stance.

- Ultimately, the anti-pattern leads to an increased organization risk profile that would be intolerable to most senior managers, had they fully understood it.

It's worth noting that you can run with this anti-pattern for years and years without discovering the negative consequences. It's only when a security incident occurs and is discovered that has substantial enough consequences to get senior management's attention that you really have to confront this anti-pattern.

It can, therefore, be a bit of a thankless task to point out that this anti-pattern is occurring, and you may not get anywhere initially. There are, nonetheless, things that should be done, as we'll discuss in our next section.

Better solutions

The solutions to this anti-pattern are fairly obvious to anyone who has spent at least a bit of time with information security. First and foremost, this is about raising awareness about the security issues that are in play and getting the internal acceptance that something needs to be done about Salesforce security in an active way, rather than assuming that the vendor will take care of it.

Some of the main points include the following:

- Engaging actively with the shared responsibility model, getting a clear understanding of where the boundaries are, how to ensure your own parts are secure, and how to continuously remain vigilant about the parts that you aren't directly responsible for but that still directly affect you.

- Investing in the required skills to perform your parts of the security task both initially and on an ongoing basis. You can build this internally or use consultants, but however you do it, the responsibility is on you to get it done.

- You need to assess new risks whenever you extend your solution in significant ways. This includes not just when you are adding new modules. Major extensions to existing functionality can also lead to new security threats being introduced.

- Fundamentally, you need to shift the mindset of your organization to one where security is seen as fundamental to organizational resilience and growth. That may be beyond what most of us as architects can accomplish. However, pushing where we can in our sphere of influence is also helpful.

- Continuously monitor your organization to evaluate Salesforce security recommendations and critical updates.

We have now completed the discussion of the first anti-pattern in this chapter and will move on to another take on the general security problem, *Compliant Is Secure*.

Mistaking other things for security

Security is a complex and multi-faceted domain. This complexity can be so profound in many cases that a strong temptation arises to simplify it to something more manageable. In this section, we will see two examples of how this can occur and what the negative consequences can be.

Compliant Is Secure

> *Compliant Is Secure holds that security for an organization can be upheld by strict adherence to one or more specified compliance regimes.*

Example

Alexandra works as an architect for LifeCo, a major provider of medical devices for the continuous measurement of vital statistics. They sell devices across a number of global markets and as a consequence are subjected to a number of different regulatory regimes. It is fair to say that a big part of LifeCo's culture is focused on meeting these regulatory requirements and maintaining compliance.

When it comes to IT security, LifeCo has also adopted a compliance-centric approach, combining ISO 27001, HIPAA, and GxP protocols in a comprehensive set of checks and controls that are documented thoroughly at the beginning of each project and audited subsequently on a yearly basis. While there are processes to maintain compliance throughout the year, LifeCo focuses most of its attention on the initial documentation and audit events.

LifeCo has adopted Salesforce for field sales and care programmes, using Sales, Service, and Health Cloud components. As part of the implementation, Alexandra worked closely with stakeholders across the business, including IT, security, legal, and the data protection office, to take Salesforce through its paces.

They performed a thorough evaluation of all the controls Salesforce has in place, both at the platform level and at the level of each individual cloud. They spent considerable time with Salesforce security representatives to understand the details of security implementation, pushing hard to get real answers to sensitive questions.

Additionally, they required comprehensive checklists and documentation from the implementation partner to ensure that all configuration work met the necessary standards. This added considerable overhead both during implementation and testing, but LifeCo was adamant that Salesforce had to meet the same standards that they apply to all internal systems.

The system documentation is finally signed off as compliant after a long period of adjustment to meet the detailed requirements. Alexandra keeps working in the Salesforce space, but mainly focuses on preparing requirements for new releases and updating technical standards unrelated to security.

Then, after 9 months, the unthinkable happens. The CEO receives a phone call from a popular news site that asks what his response is to the fact that thousands of the company's patients' personal information has been dumped online on a dark website. There is no doubt that the data comes from LifeCo, as it contains company proprietary information about device usage.

The CEO articulates a rushed response, but the damage is done. LifeCo suffers a major blow to its reputation and is battered in the mainstream media, social media, and the stock market. Alexandra takes a leading role in the investigation and cleanup after the incident.

The investigation is not entirely conclusive, but there is good circumstantial evidence pointing toward a disgruntled employee exporting a report file with the personal information and uploading it online. There isn't enough evidence to bring any formal charges, however.

The root-cause analysis concludes that the incident occurred because a special procedure to give users reporting rights to patient data had been used to extend the privileges to a team of 50 people, many quite junior and relatively untrained in IT security or compliance. This had been done with the blessing of several senior managers to work around a number of management-reporting issues in the system. By exporting and manually processing the data in Excel, the team was able to compensate for certain functional shortcomings in the Salesforce implementation.

The problem is remediated, and an investigation is done to find other similar cases where a process might have been used to circumvent good practice. At audit time, Salesforce passes the audit with no serious reservations. However, in Alexandra's mind, there still lingers a doubt that maybe they never really got to the bottom of the issue.

Problem

You might be tempted to think that the problem that *Compliant Is Secure* seeks to resolve is the same as for *Shared Belongs to Salesforce* – that is to say, what the anti-pattern seeks to resolve is the general security problem of how to keep data and systems secure. That is, however, subtly wrong.

While our last anti-pattern sought to solve security in general, *Compliant Is Secure* sidesteps the problem of actually being secure with the practices required to demonstrate to certain external parties that you are secure – that is to say, the documentation and checklists become the point rather than the actual security practices they are meant to encourage.

This is similar to *Shared Belongs to Salesforce* in so far as we reduce the complex, wicked problem of actually staying secure by replacing it with the much simpler problem of ticking all the right boxes. The strategy of reducing cognitive load by simplifying to a set of well-understood, repeatable processes, as we'll see in the next section, is quite attractive to certain kinds of organizations.

Proposed solution

Compliant Is Secure proposes to substitute and thereby resolve the problem of keeping systems and data secure with the simpler problem of staying compliant with a set of clearly defined standards. That way, you can move forward in confidence that you have followed good practice and, therefore, are as secure as you are likely to get.

A good image to keep in mind for this anti-pattern is a checklist.

Let's be very clear – compliance is a great thing! You should absolutely be compliant with the standards that define good practice in your industry and in general. This applies to information security, and it applies in general.

Compliance with standards can be an extremely good way to encourage good practice within your organization and embed it within its culture. What makes this scenario an anti-pattern is that compliance becomes the end goal, whereas that should, in fact, be the awareness and improvement in practice that the compliance exercise is meant to encourage.

Put another way, with information security, you should aim to use compliance as a tool to become more secure and more security-aware, not as a way to get security out of the way because you've ticked all the boxes. It is, however, not difficult to understand why it is attractive to organizations to focus principally on compliance:

- Compliance turns the fuzzy and wicked problem of information security into a manageable and governable one. Managers tend to like problems that are easy to understand and clearly measurable. Compliance is easy to understand; security is not.

- The processes needed to establish and maintain compliance tend to fit well with existing processes and skills, especially in companies that operate in regulated industries such as life sciences or the defense sector.

- When things go wrong, you have clear and unambiguous documentation that you have followed the rules. That helps both in terms of explaining incidents externally and protecting relevant stakeholders internally.

- You have to stay compliant anyway. For most large organizations, a certain level of compliance is mandatory and embedded in law or industry standards. Given that you have to be compliant, there is a clear temptation to make that the end goal.

The results you get from falling into this anti-pattern, however, are frequently problematic, as we'll discuss in our next section.

Results

What you achieve with the *Compliant Is Secure* anti-pattern is, generally speaking, point-in-time compliance to a standard. You will be compliant at each audit point, and in between, people will follow the necessary processes that are required from them.

However, you have not instituted any deeper sense of the importance of security within the organization or given people the training and tools to engage meaningfully with it. That means that you will often find many workarounds, such as the one described in our example, where people do something that is technically compliant but completely circumvents the spirit of security that inspired the rules of the compliance standard.

You often see two patterns emerge in compliance-centric organizations:

- **Drift and remediation**: In this pattern, you have an ongoing drift away from the standards that have been implemented because people see compliance as a point-in-time exercise. This is corrected periodically to bring the organization back into compliance during an audit.

- **Structured circumvention**: In this pattern, you continuously follow the rules, but you have included within your compliance system certain ways of granting exceptions, which get exploited systematically to make the life of workers within the organization easier in one way or another. This is the pattern we saw in the preceding example.

Fundamentally, with the *Compliant Is Secure* anti-pattern, your organization is missing the "why" of security. They are doing certain things to check the boxes but do not engage with them beyond that exercise. That points toward the key interventions that will help with this pattern, which we'll discuss next.

Better solutions

There is a famous book by business author Simon Sinek called *Start with Why*. In it, Sinek posits that the most successful organizations, Apple being the canonical example, do not start with what products they are selling, or how they make them, but with a fundamental purpose expressed in an answer to why the company exists in the first place.

While I won't make any comments on the merits of this position relative to business in general, when it comes to information security, it is entirely correct. The reason why *Compliant Is Secure* is an anti-pattern is because it neglects the underlying "why" of information security.

The cure to this problem is, of course, to start from the answer to "why" – keeping information secure is not only essential to avoid threats but actually enables an organization to remain resilient and grow in a safe manner. Then, you can move on to the how and what of compliance regimes and specific controls.

That is a big mouthful for most Salesforce professionals to take on. Helpfully, there are smaller more practical things that we can also do to help:

- Continuously make other stakeholders aware that ticking boxes does not mean that the organization will remain secure

- Train people in Salesforce security and the threats that can occur despite the compliance regime

- Find champions to take on security awareness on an ongoing basis

- Advocate for ongoing monitoring of the Salesforce organization at the security level by these trained and motivated people

- Spread knowledge and awareness throughout the organization by regularly bringing up the topic at meetings and dedicated sessions

Of course, also remember that compliance is important, and you should do your part to stay compliant. Having now considered a very general security anti-pattern, we will once again focus on a specific Salesforce security anti-pattern, *Declarative Is Always Safe*.

Declarative Is Always Safe

> *Falling into the Declarative Is Always Safe anti-pattern implies having an over-optimistic attitude toward the security of declarative customization features.*

Example

Rakesh is the technical lead for Salesforce at BigCo. BigCo is a long-term user of Salesforce with a big footprint across half a dozen different clouds. They expanded usage massively during the COVID-19 pandemic to facilitate a number of processes being carried out remotely.

Rakesh and his team worked with several smaller partners on the creation of these processes. Because of the time pressure involved, they built the processes using a combination of out-of-the-box features and flows, leaving out any complex requirements for a later time. The flow-based approach was recommended by the architects both from a speed-of-development and security perspective.

With the cooperation of the business, this approach proved adequate as a stopgap measure and BigCo managed the transition to remote work relatively seamlessly, partly due to this work. After the initial release, Rakesh and the team kept working on improving and elaborating the new flows, and some have evolved into complex, multi-faceted business applications with powerful features to support the business.

This includes the ability to make mass updates, creations, and deletions, the ability to call other systems via APIs, and even the ability to grant new security features to employees when they take on new roles or responsibilities in the business. There are also administrative flows that Super Users can use to manage the backend functions.

Functionally, this works well for the business, but on several occasions, mistakes by users lead to accidental record deletion. When a particularly unlucky Super User by accident deletes a large number of opportunities using an administrative flow, the CTO decides to have a partner review the flows, as he's worried about any potential wider issues.

The partner does a review of the flows and comes back with a long list of unsafe practices used in the flows. In particular, the flows give system administrator-level access to a very large number of users that do not have the requisite training to use them. That presents not only an issue of accidental deletion, which has already happened, but also a real security issue. That includes threats both from malicious employees and from external threat agents, as some of the flows are theoretically triggerable via API updates.

The harm from the incident is easily remedied, as BigCo has an advanced backup solution in place, but the remediation of the flows takes much longer. For all future development, Rakesh works with the external partner to create a clear set of security guidelines to be followed when creating flows.

Problem

The problem that *Declarative Is Always Safe* seeks to solve is that of secure development or customization – that is to say, how do we keep our code and customizations from creating vulnerabilities that can be exploited to get at our data and systems?

It isn't surprising that there is a tendency to consider low-code or no-code approaches as a cure for security headaches. Many classic and well-advertised vulnerabilities have been down to obscure coding errors, so avoiding code seems like a good idea if you want to be more secure.

Of course, low-code/no-code approaches are relatively recent phenomena, so whether this will hold well in practice is still up in the air to some extent. The reasoning is generally sound, however, as vendors such as Salesforce will spend much more time securing the low-code components they make available than you can spend on your own code.

However, as we will see when we cover the detail of the proposed solution next, this reasoning is not airtight.

Proposed solution

The proposed solution to the problem of secure development and configuration that *Declarative Is Always Safe* proposes is to circumvent the problem by only using declarative features – for example, custom objects, page layouts, flows, and even OmniStudio – which are assumed to be secure by default. That way, we do not have to spend much time thinking about security, and we can get our features done quicker.

This is clearly an attractive proposition to many different stakeholders:

- First, it is partially true. Low-code approaches are less likely, all things equal, than code-based ones to contain security gaps.

- Second, it simplifies development and configuration by putting clear bounds around what can be configured.

- Third, it provides the technical team with a good way to push back on business requirements that are too complex.

- Fourth, it speeds up the delivery of features by leveraging pre-built functionality that can be adapted to your particular business need.

A focus on declarative features, then, brings many benefits with it and is usually considered a good practice within the Salesforce community. However, what can make this focus – if taken too far – a security anti-pattern is the blindness to the very real threats that can be present, even in declarative solutions.

Results

The key negative result from the *Declarative Is Always Safe* anti-pattern, then, is blindness to security threats that may be present in your solution and a lack of awareness that such threats might even be there. This can lead to serious negative consequences, as in the previous example. The problem, however, is only getting worse day by day as Salesforce brings out new declarative features.

It is clear from the way features are being released on the Salesforce platform that Salesforce wants low-code tools such as Flow and OmniStudio to be the go-to solutioning toolkits for customization on the platform. However, the more powerful these tools become, the more likely you will be able to do something that will result in a security issue.

Let's, for instance, consider some security problems that can happen with flows:

- General permissions such as **Run Flows** or the **Flow User** license can give a very large number of users permissions to run all flows in an organization, leading to issues such as those in our example

- If users have access to the **AllFlows** list view, they can then run any flow in the organization from the UI; this includes external users

- Flow execution contexts are complex to understand, and it is easy to end up running a flow in system mode by mistake, leading to a potential escalation of user rights

- Client-side validation in flows can accidentally leak information in some cases by including data in the response

- Component visibility can leak information, as the component is still included in the HTTP response

- Apex actions with wide-ranging effects may be called from flows without a clear understanding of the security implications

I recommend the article *Understanding Salesforce Flows and Common Security Risks*, available at `https://appomni.com/resources/aolabs/understanding-salesforce-flows-and-common-security-risks/`, as a good introduction to some common flow issues.

However, the wider point is that there are real security issues that happen with flows, OmniStudio, and even simpler declarative features. Therefore, we cannot rely on them to be safe by default, but we have to take due precautions, which we'll discuss in our next section.

Better solutions

The first and most important piece of advice for avoiding this anti-pattern is to treat your declarative solutions every bit as seriously as you would your code-based ones. Tools such as flows or OmniStudio are increasingly as powerful as Apex and solve similarly complex business requirements.

That means you should follow a software development process for solutions based on these tools that are fit for purpose, just as you would for a code-based solution. Specifically, when it comes to security, you should keep the following things in mind:

- Standards and guidelines for declarative solutions should be in place as they would be if you were writing code

- Conduct risk and threat assessments at the start of the project for declarative solutions that deal with sensitive data or deploy a lot of power

- Train developers and configurators to understand the issues, and create a general awareness about what relying on declarative tools does and does not accomplish

- Keep an eye on the long-term trend toward declarative tools and update your guidelines as needed

- Monitor the external environment for issues or exploits related to declarative functionality on Salesforce

With that said, we will finish our discussion of security-related anti-patterns by taking a look at how you can really muck up your sharing model in Salesforce.

Sharing isn't always caring

Salesforce has one of the most powerful and complicated sharing architectures known to man. This is both a blessing and a curse. In this section, however, we will focus on showing how it can go wrong and what to do to prevent it.

Spaghetti Sharing Model

A Spaghetti Sharing Model does to the security of a Salesforce organization what spaghetti code does to the maintainability of an application.

Example

GlobalCo is a conglomerate with numerous different business lines selling products across a number of B2B verticals. Most of GlobalCo's organization is run within the business units, but IT has become a strong global function, as it has made it possible to collaborate effectively across business units using simple tools such as Slack for collaboration.

A few years back, GlobalCo adopted Salesforce Sales and Service clouds as their corporate CRM. Huan was the lead architect on that project and now sits in the global Salesforce Center of Excellence. While some subsidiaries still use other CRMs operationally, all basic data about customer transactions must make its way to Salesforce. To encourage standardization of processes and data, GlobalCo adopted a strong single organizational strategy for its Salesforce environment.

Unfortunately, while GlobalCo would like to be able to share as much data as possible globally, a number of regulations prevent it from going as far as it would like. There are a number of problems:

- Some countries require their data to be isolated from others, creating country data silos

- Competition law in a variety of jurisdictions also prevents some subsidiaries from sharing data with specific other subsidiaries to prevent collusion

- Salespeople in some jurisdictions are near-paranoid about who can see their opportunities, fearing someone else will steal them, leading to a number of extra protections being put in place

- Finally, executives in certain business units are used to keeping sensitive opportunities and customer support cases secret and only sharing among a select few, which has also been at least partially accommodated

After going live, there have been a lot of complaints that the structure GlobalCo put in place to meet these requirements was excessively rigid. There is a call for a number of exceptions from at least half a dozen countries.

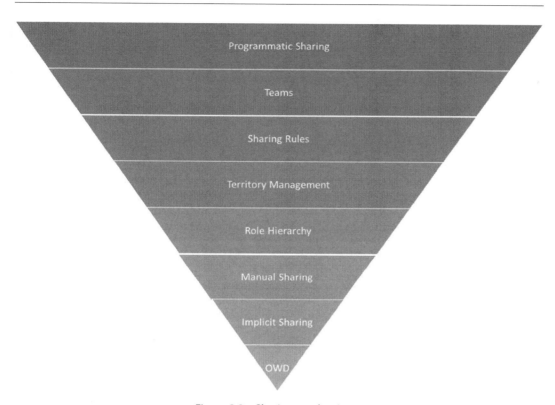

Figure 3.2 – Sharing mechanisms

Huan leads the team to investigate the requirements. Initially, he thinks the problem is solvable by making minor adjustments to the organizational hierarchy and enterprise territory management. This, however, proves too simplistic, and he devises a number of additional public groups to make more refinements to the model.

Users, however, are still complaining, so Huan gets creative with the use of the account and opportunity teams. However, because the process needed would be too onerous to manage manually, the team ends up implementing a number of automations to automatically add team members to account and opportunity teams, based on certain criteria.

Even that, however, turns out to not be able to capture the full extent of the business requirements for when certain records should and shouldn't be shared between specified business units and countries. Huan specifies an Apex-based sharing mechanism and gives it to a development team to implement.

The complete adjustment to the sharing model goes live, globally, over a weekend. Smoke testing is fine, but everyone is holding their breath as the testing of the model is difficult, and no one has been able to definitively say that all the important scenarios have been tested.

While there is no disaster, a steady trickle of access issues makes its way to the team over the week following the go-live. There are a lot of cases where either someone has access that shouldn't have, or someone lacks access they should have.

What's much worse, however, is that the team is finding it nearly impossible to pinpoint the errors. There are just so many moving parts that figuring out what is going wrong in specific cases becomes too complex. Every time the team thinks they have fixed one issue, it seems another two appear as a consequence.

After several frustrating weeks of trying to resolve the problem, the change management board takes a decision to roll back the changes to the sharing model and find a set of manual workarounds, until a more stable technical solution can be found.

Problem

In classical software applications, there is a well-known concept called **spaghetti code**. It happens when programmers work without design, practices, or the necessary experience to implement a system. Instead, they just do one thing at a time in a way that works for now with no consideration of the bigger picture.

Over time, this leads to code that resembles a portion of spaghetti on a plate. Everything is tangled up with everything else, changes to one part of the system impact other parts in seemingly random ways, and even the original writers of the code don't really understand what is going on.

Happily, on Salesforce, we rarely see spaghetti code to this extent. It can occur, but in my experience, it is quite rare. What does occur frequently are *Spaghetti Sharing Models* – that is to say, sharing models that are so complicated that even their designers can't reliably tell in a specific case why someone has or hasn't got access to a given record.

The *Spaghetti Sharing Model* anti-pattern arises from an honest attempt to give a business what it wants in terms of record sharing. The problem is that for large global organizations, the level of complexity experienced in this area is so large that it is nearly impossible to get right.

In our example, we saw some of the reasons why:

- Privacy laws differ between countries and determine what can and cannot be shared

- Competition law can restrict visibility between subsidiaries

- Concerns about bonuses and commissions are extremely important to sales teams and can lead to serious concerns about data sharing

- Executives often want to keep certain data secret for a variety of business reasons, while sharing other data that is less sensitive of the same type

There are more scenarios than these, concerning, for instance, protection of sensitive health or financial data according to certain laws and standards, or internal political factors within an organization that may impact sharing requirements.

Overall, if you find yourself in an organization with this kind of requirements setup for data sharing, you are in danger of ending up in the *Spaghetti Sharing Model* anti-pattern, simply by trying to accommodate the requirements you are given.

Proposed solution

The *Spaghetti Sharing Model* anti-pattern suggests that you address sharing requirements in an incremental, iterative way, seeking as closely as possible to meet the business need.

This seems eminently sensible because of the following:

- It is exactly what we would do for most other types of requirements
- It fits with the dominant agile approaches to software development that are used by most Salesforce implementation teams
- You can nearly always achieve your goal in the short term
- It takes a long time before the complexity reaches a level to make the process go off the rails

Unfortunately, this process can break down in organizations of a certain size and complexity, resulting in the anti-pattern we are discussing, as we'll see in the next section.

Results

The result of the *Spaghetti Sharing Model* is a situation where some or more of the following characteristics are present:

- Records are shared with some users without anyone fully understanding why
- Record access is missing from some users without anyone fully understanding why
- Pinpointing access issues is extremely difficult
- Making changes to the sharing model is either considered entirely off limits due to complexity
- Changes to sharing often lead to new issues that are difficult to understand and fix

It is worth reflecting on why sharing is more prone to spaghetti than other configuration areas. The answer lies mostly in the vast number of mechanisms that are available to control sharing on Salesforce and their interactions. Depending on how you count, there are more than 20 different ways to extend the sharing of objects and records in Salesforce.

The following table shows a sample of mechanisms that can be used to control sharing:

Mechanism	What it's used for
Ownership	Access to a record owner, user, or queue
Profile	Access to an object or not at the basic level
Permission Set	Access to an object or not at the basic level
Org-Wide Default (Internal)	Default internal sharing level
Org-Wide Default (External)	Default external sharing level
Role Hierarchy	Access to subordinates' records
Grant Access Using Hierarchies	Sharing with a role hierarchy or not
Public Groups	Sharing to a defined group of users
Ownership-Based Sharing Rule	Sharing based on a configured rule, based on record ownership
Criteria-Based Sharing Rule	Sharing based on a configured rule, based on record field values
Guest User Sharing Rule	Special sharing to the guest user
Account Teams	Sharing based on membership in an account team
Opportunity Teams	Sharing based on membership in an opportunity team
Case Teams	Sharing based on membership in a case team
Manual Sharing	Sharing records manually
Implicit Sharing	Automated sharing between parents and children for certain standard objects
Territory Hierarchy	Sharing based on configured territories and territory membership
External Account Hierarchy	Grant access based on account hierarchy
Sharing Group	Sharing records owned by portal users
Sharing Set	Sharing records to portal users based on matches between Account or Contact fields
Manager Groups	Sharing records with our management chain
Apex Sharing	Sharing programmatically

Table 3.1

Ultimately, this vast number of mechanisms, if used injudiciously, can lead to the *Spaghetti Sharing model*, simply because their interaction becomes difficult for a human brain to understand.

Better solutions

As we have seen, the *Spaghetti Sharing Model* can occur just by people doing their job and incrementally seeking to create value for the business by meeting their requirements. That means this anti-pattern can occur without anyone doing anything wrong or making a specifically wrong decision. Someone needs to step outside of their day-to-day remit in order to spot this issue prior to it occurring.

At the risk of provoking severe retaliation from agile fundamentalists, I will suggest that if you find yourself in an organization (where there are highly complex sharing requirements), you need to stop, take a step back, and put in place an upfront design for the sharing architecture along with governance mechanisms to enforce it over time. For instance, you might introduce a principle that it is best to be parsimonious in using sharing mechanisms, and make the adoption of new types of sharing subject to approval by an architecture review board or design authority.

This concludes our presentation of security anti-patterns. We will now look at the key things to take away from the discussion.

Knowing the takeaways

In this section, we will abstract a bit from the specific patterns and instead try to pull out the wider learning points you can use in your day-to-day work as a Salesforce architect or in preparing for the CTA Review Board.

When architecting Salesforce solutions, you should be mindful of the following:

- Security is not just a technical issue; the way you frame problems and create awareness is even more important.

- It is easy to ignore complex security issues in various ways. While you may not be able to singlehandedly change this as an architect, you can be a part of raising awareness.

- Instituting sharing sessions and sending out relevant material is one good way you can help make things better.

- You can also ensure that security guidelines and practices on a technical level reflect the full threat picture.

- Do not assume that something is Salesforce's responsibility without good evidence.

- Do not assume that because you are using a declarative feature, you cannot have a security gap.

- Find ways of monitoring the security stance of your Salesforce organizations on a regular basis and act on the intelligence.

- Make security matters a recurring discussion in governance forums where you can influence the agenda.

- Don't build sharing models incrementally unless your requirements are very simple.

- Instead, take the pain upfront and come up with a set of mechanisms that can work in your scenario.

In preparing for the CTA Review Board, you should be mindful of the following:

- Security is embedded in a lot of areas, so even though it is a distinct domain, you should still cover security matters concisely when relevant in your solution run-through.

- Security is a complex area, so be as clear and concise as possible. It is very easy to get drawn into long discussions on security matters and you don't have the time for that at a review board.

- Consider including some comments on security when reviewing your governance model and potential risks.

- Be parsimonious when picking security mechanisms. Fewer mechanisms are easier to explain and less likely to have interactions that lead to unforeseen consequences.

- Of course, don't oversimplify or make assumptions that would point in the direction of not appreciating how things can go wrong in the security domain.

- Sharing is particularly easy to get wrong, so be quite careful about designing exotic sharing solutions.

- Don't invent additional security requirements that aren't stated in the scenario. You can easily think yourself into additional implied requirements when reading many scenarios.

- The one exception to this rule is dealing with privacy laws, such as **General Data Protection Regulation (GDPR)**, if you have an organization in a jurisdiction where it applies.

We have now covered the material for this chapter and are ready to proceed. First, however, we will summarize what we have learned.

Summary

In this chapter, we have seen how there are many ways to compromise your security by following seemingly innocuous courses of action or failing to realize subtle distinctions in responsibilities and approaches.

These included both general security anti-patterns that affect many different platforms, such as *Shared Belongs to Salesforce* and *Compliant Is Secure*, and unique Salesforce anti-patterns such as *Declarative Is Always Safe* and *Spaghetti Sharing Model*. That underscores the particular complexity of the security domain.

When it comes to security, you have to attend both to high-level issues of organizational culture and awareness of issues, and to the minutiae of how mechanisms are designed specifically for the technology you are using. That is what makes it both frustrating and highly interesting at the same time.

Having covered the security domain, we will move on to have a look at data next.

4

What Not to Do about Data

This chapter is about the ways in which you can compromise your data layer on the Salesforce platform. Throughout this chapter, we cover four data domain anti-patterns that occur with some frequency in Salesforce environments and give you pointers on how to recognize and avoid them.

In this chapter, we're going to cover the following main topics:

- Why treating Salesforce as a relational database won't lead to acceptable results
- How failing to coordinate activities can lead to a disconnected data model with serious negative repercussions
- The negative consequences of failing to plan for growth in your database, especially when you should know better
- Why data synchronization can be a great solution on a small scale, but a nightmare on a larger scale

After completing this chapter, you will have a good understanding of how Salesforce is different from a traditional relational database and why that matters greatly. You will also know the importance of good governance, planning for data modeling and growth, and what can go wrong when you don't have governance in place. Finally, you will have a deeper insight into the complexities of data synchronization.

Mistaking Salesforce for a regular database

Many people come to the Salesforce ecosystem from other technology backgrounds, and they often come with preconceptions about how architecture should be done based on their past experiences. While that can be enriching to the platform, there are also cases where it can lead you to go astray, architecturally speaking. Perhaps the most frequent of these is the mistake of using Salesforce as though it were some other kind of database—generally a relational one.

Salesforce as Relational Database

The Salesforce as Relational Database anti-pattern consists of mistaking the Salesforce data layer for a relational database.

Example

UmbrellaCo is the largest global manufacturer of umbrellas for the tourism industry. They use Salesforce for managing their B2B sales channel, including opportunity management, quoting, and ordering.

However, in the overall systems landscape within UmbrellaCo, Salesforce is a relatively minor component. Overall, the landscape is dominated by a set of bespoke lines of business systems that have been developed and maintained in-house and an aging **Manufacturing Resource Planning (MRP)** system.

There is also a relatively modern middleware platform and UmbrellaCo's approach to Enterprise IT that relies heavily on integrating, translating, and combining data from various systems within the middleware. This allows them some additional agility that they otherwise would not be able to have, given their aging and bespoke systems portfolio.

Rishi is the responsible manager for Salesforce at UmbrellaCo. He is an external hire that only recently joined the company from a mid-size ecosystem partner. One of the first things he has to deal with settling into his new role is a series of complaints from the middleware team about the Salesforce data model.

UmbrellaCo has longstanding practices for modeling certain kinds of data such as different types of accounts, for example, SME accounts versus large corporate accounts, and strict standards for modeling addresses. The Salesforce model does not accommodate this model in the standard way, leading to substantial work on the middleware team in mapping the data to other systems.

John, an integration architect long employed by UmbrellaCo, is assigned to the Salesforce team in order to align the Salesforce data model. Rishi is immediately quite uncomfortable in the collaboration with John. John displays a high degree of distaste for the Salesforce data model and thinks it fundamentally fails to conform to good data modeling practices.

The standard within UmbrellaCo is to use relational databases, normalized to **Third Normal Form (3NF)**, and follow the corporate conventions for key data types. Salesforce does not meet these expectations and cannot easily be made to do so. Rishi tries to explain that the Salesforce data model shouldn't be thought of as a classical relational database, whatever superficial resemblance it might have to one, but his objections fall on deaf ears.

After a month of work, John puts forward his proposal for reworking the Salesforce data model. It involves replacing the standard Salesforce address field with a new set of custom objects incorporating the address and an arbitrary number of address lines linked to the master account object. Different types of accounts will get their own individual custom objects and refer back to the master account object using an inheritance-like interface.

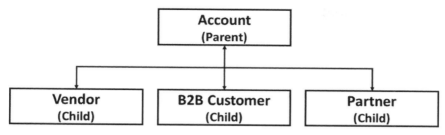

Figure 4.1 – Proposal for refactoring account model

This will require both rework on the user interface and an internal data migration exercise within Salesforce to accomplish, but John is adamant that this will bring the system into line with corporate standards and make life easier on the middleware team.

Rishi vehemently objects and even gets his Salesforce account executive to bring in a senior solution engineer from Salesforce, trying to explain why following this plan is a surefire way to cripple the Salesforce platform and make additional projects more complex and expensive. The objections make their way to the company's architecture forum but are rejected as conformance to corporate standards is considered a more important imperative.

Going forward, data modeling on Salesforce should follow the normal UmbrellaCo standards and deliver well-normalized data models that meet the specifications set out in the enterprise data model. Rishi draws a deep breath and consigns himself to having to do mostly bespoke solutions on Salesforce going forward.

Problem

The problem addressed by Salesforce as Relational Database is the general one of modeling business entities in the context of a software system. In this case, use the most commonly used modeling paradigm in the software industry: relational database models.

In this approach, you map a logical model of a business domain into a set of database tables, using a process called **normalization**. The details of what normalization is do not need to concern us much, but it is fundamentally concerned with the elimination of redundancy within the database. That is to say, each piece of information should be held once and uniquely within the database and then referenced in all of the places that it's used.

In addition, there should not be repeating fields, such as multiple address lines, and all the fields in an entity should rely explicitly on the primary key: the ID field in Salesforce. You should always have one and only one unique key for the entity.

By applying these and a few more elaborate rules with greater or lesser stringency, you get to a certain normal form, the name for models of normalization. The strictest application is something called **Sixth Normal Form** (6NF) where you end up with tables consisting of only a primary key and one other attribute. However, most enterprise applications strive for something called 3NF, which effectively meets the criteria we outlined above.

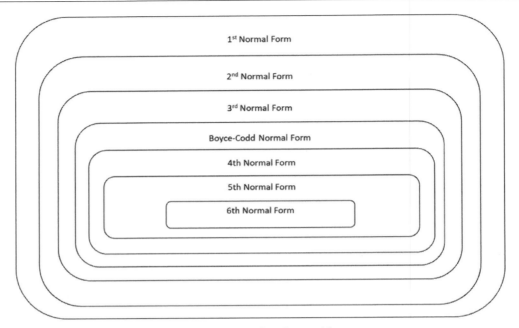

Figure 4.2 – Hierarchy of normal forms

This is all well and good and is the accepted way to do things for systems based on relational databases. However, Salesforce, while it has a number of surface similarities to a relational database (namely tables, called objects) and relationships (in the form of lookup and master/detail relationships that enable its use as a relational database), is not a relational database and should not be treated as such.

Proposed solution

Salesforce as Relational Database ignores the distinctive nature of the data modeling used on the Salesforce platform and replaces it with a model that bases itself on relational databases. This means using custom objects freely to serve as tables and relationships of either type to serve as foreign key relations.

It explicitly ignores Salesforce's standard ways of dealing with record differentiation, such as record types and page layouts, in favor of a relational model with a larger number of unique custom objects. In addition, this anti-pattern tends to make scant use of standard objects as these do not fit with a well-normalized data model.

This solution makes a lot of sense to many experienced architects coming to Salesforce from other platforms without a lot of understanding or training. It is, after all, the accepted way for things to be done in all traditional enterprise systems, and consistency with an accepted standard is extremely valuable in enterprise architecture.

However, bending a system so out of shape as this pattern does to Salesforce goes to show that every standard has exceptions.

Results

As we saw in the earlier example, the result of introducing this anti-pattern is fundamentally increasing the complexity of your Salesforce solution, resulting in additional costs both for solutioning and maintenance.

By relying on custom objects for nearly everything, you reduce your ability to leverage out-of-the-box features, because relational models tend to require a larger number of smaller objects, which makes some commonly used Salesforce features (for example, cross-object reporting or cross-object formula fields) nearly impossible to use.

That means you'll most likely need to write more custom code or construct complex custom flows, which is where you take a real hit both on upfront implementation cost and time and on the maintenance and extensibility of the solution afterward.

There is also the opportunity cost of not being able to use standard functionality to the same extent and not being able to adopt newly released features with the same frequency to consider. All in all, this is a high price to pay for consistency.

Better solutions

The data domain is an area where you should adopt the Salesforce way to get the best results. While sometimes there are exceptions to Salesforce good practices, when it comes to data modeling, the guidance should be followed nearly without exceptions.

That means modeling broad-based business objects directly in the system rather than going through a normalization process and relying on the platform to manage and optimize the data or at least give you the tools to do so. It also means using standard objects whenever you can, avoiding Custom Objects whenever possible, and ensuring that the data model is well governed to avoid issues with data integrity and redundancy.

This is obvious to many people who have grown their careers in the Salesforce ecosystem, but it is counterintuitive to most traditional architects. This, then, is one of the few anti-patterns that is more likely to be initiated by a highly experienced architect than a brand new one. It's also more common in AppExchange applications than in standard implementations as these are closer to the traditional development models found on other platforms.

Forgetting about governance

Governance is important in all architecture domains, but perhaps a few domains can go wrong where governance is missing as the data domain. In the following sections, we will explore two examples of this phenomenon, starting with what happens when you fail to coordinate data models on a common platform.

Disconnected Entities

Disconnected Entities is an anti-pattern characterized by unconnected data entities proliferating in a common database, often with multiple database representations of the same business level entity.

Example

SmileCo is a major provider of dental supplies operating in several global cities. They have been using Salesforce for several years, using a departmental strategy, where each department has run independently on Salesforce without central oversight.

There are three departments that use Salesforce in a serious way and they are as follows:

- **Finance**, which uses it for debt collection using a home-grown application
- **Logistics**, which uses it for vendor management using an application that has been developed by a small ecosystem partner
- **Sales**, which uses a standard Sales Cloud implementation

The information in these apps is spread out and there is no cross-visibility or collaboration between the teams. Kimmy is a consulting manager at a Salesforce Summit partner who is brought in with a small team to enable a comprehensive view of the underlying data.

She, however, soon discovers that the job is bigger than she bargained for. The finance application uses a flat, denormalized data model to model debt collection. All information is held in a giant debt custom object, including all contact and account information. This data is not validated and data quality at a glance seems problematic.

The logistics application effectively mirrors the standard Salesforce data model using custom objects to represent vendors, vendor contacts, and information about quotes and purchases made from vendors. The fields differ substantially from the standard Salesforce data model but could be made to fit with standard objects such as account and contact with a bit of creative data mapping.

The Sales Cloud implementation is relatively standard but uses quite a few additional custom fields that in no way match up with the way data is modeled in the other two platform apps. Kimmy reports her findings to the client, who after some hesitation requests that she continues with a plan for consolidation nonetheless.

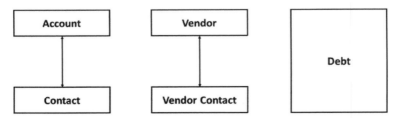

Figure 4.3 – Three different ways of representing account and contact

The plan she proposes seeks to standardize the use of the Account and Contact objects, using the standard objects, across all three departments, and on that basis write a set of reports and dashboards giving the required overview. She gives up on trying to consolidate additional objects as they are too far away from any standard objects for the attempt to be likely to succeed.

For the finance application, she suggests renormalizing the account and contact parts of the gigantic debt object. This requires a data migration exercise as well as significant work to deduplicate and improve data quality. Rework on the application itself, thankfully, is relatively minor due to the simple declarative features used for its implementation.

The logistics application presents a larger problem. Most of the functionality is in custom code and requires substantial rework. The partner is reluctant to make the changes Kimmy suggested as they prefer working in their own space, but after some pushing, they relent. However, the changes are quite expensive and take several months to implement.

Overall, what was meant to be a small consulting engagement of a few weeks' duration ends up taking more than three months, incurring substantial costs. Upon leaving the client, Kimmy sends a new proposal for introducing some basic Salesforce governance functions within SmileCo. They take the proposal under advisement and promise to get back to Kimmy in good time.

Problem

Disconnected Entities is another anti-pattern that happens when you fail to recognize that certain practices carried out without oversight or governance can result in serious issues at a higher level of operation. It is caused by a lack of awareness rather than by the attempt to achieve something specific.

It tends to occur in smaller or highly decentralized organizations where different groups may share the same infrastructure, in this case a Salesforce org, but not really coordinate activities beyond the absolute basics. It also requires an environment where IT maturity is low and governance of IT is minimal.

Proposed solution

So far as we can frame what the Disconnected Entities anti-pattern proposes as a solution, it effectively says something along the lines of don't worry about the data model, any design will be good enough. At least that is how it will be interpreted because there will be no standards, practices, or guidelines to follow.

Lack of governance can have bad effects in many domains, but in the data domain, the Disconnected Entities anti-pattern is one of the worst. It means that teams build in isolation with no awareness of what else exists on the same platform or how other teams are using the same elements (even the same standard objects).

That means that you can have a cross-organizational impact without realizing it. And at the very least, the anti-pattern leads to the kind of scenario sketched in our earlier example where cross-departmental initiatives are hampered or blocked by the data model.

Results

For the Disconnected Entities anti-pattern, the results can be as chaotic as the process that produces them. For the small teams whose uncoordinated work eventually causes the anti-pattern, it usually works out just fine in the short term.

When you are working in isolation on your own thing, there really isn't any short-term impact to doing things badly or idiosyncratically. The impact only comes with scale, coordination requirements, or a need to extend the application to new use cases.

The specific negative consequences can therefore vary considerably, but some common ones include the following:

- An inability to achieve 360-degree visibility of contacts or accounts, or any other relevant business entity for that matter
- An inability to do cross-departmental or cross-application reporting
- Increased cost of new development and maintenance due to variability and complexity in the data layer
- An inability to connect applications or create cross-departmental workflows without incurring substantial rework costs to bring different areas in line with each other
- Duplication of effort between different areas
- Less scope for adopting new standard features as they are released because of inconsistencies in the data models

Overall, then, this anti-pattern has many of the same characteristics in the data domain that Big Ball of Mud had in the system domain or that Spaghetti Sharing Model had in the security domain.

Better solutions

Unsurprisingly, the key to avoiding an anti-pattern caused by missing governance and awareness is to institute the appropriate governance- and awareness-generating mechanisms. That means first and foremost having the appropriate governance forums in place, where different areas can coordinate their activities in a structured way.

This needs to be supported by good data governance standards and practices to support the work done in the relevant forums. These can take different forms depending on the organization and its culture, but to avoid Disconnected Entities, a list such as the following is a starting point:

- Rigidly enforce the use of standard objects and fields wherever possible
- Ensure that teams use standard objects and fields consistently
- Have an approval process for creating new custom objects that teams must follow

- Have a lighter approval process for creating custom fields

- Define ownership of all objects and ensure that object owners are consulted about all changes to their objects

- Have an architect or two take a global view of the data model and offer ongoing advice on its evolution

Having now covered what happens when you fail to coordinate your activities in the data domain, we will move on to look at what can happen if you fail to plan for growth.

Unplanned Growth

> *The Unplanned Growth anti-pattern happens when organizations fail to plan for growth in the data to be stored, although they could or should have known better.*

Example

HappyWorkoutCo is a sportswear retailer with more than 200 shops globally. They have developed a customized retail management application based on Salesforce Industries but with a large amount of customization and some bespoke development. The application has been developed in an agile, iterative fashion and that is also the way they are proposing to go live.

Martin is in charge of the rollout to the stores. Initially, they will roll out the product for only three small product categories to a handful of stores in major markets. While the product tests well, Martin still has butterflies as the first stores go live.

But this time, the rollout is a great success. The product works flawlessly and the staff in the stores loves the new capabilities the software gives them for greater individual engagement with customers across channels.

Buoyed by the initial success, Martin and his team start a program of incremental rollouts to both more stores and product categories. Everything initially continues to go well, but after a while, complaints start coming in about system performance. There is a noticeable slowdown on a number of screens in the system and some key reports take minutes to run.

A task force consisting of members of Martin's team as well as technical resources from the development partner is put together to have a look at the issue. However, the decision is made to continue the rollout of both new products and new stores.

The task force gets underway, but soon after it begins its work, a major incident occurs following a major go-live where 20 new shops and several thousands of products were being brought online. The system creeps to a halt and several screens stop working altogether.

Martin's team conducts an emergency rollback, which restores the system to an operational state, but now all eyes are on the performance task force. The team works quickly with renewed vigor and intensity and discovers what it believes to be the root cause.

Inside the package containing the core retail management application, there is a junction object that contains a record for each product configuration available at a given retail store. When the system went live there were five stores, 100 products, and about ten configurations each, for a total of 5,000 records.

After the big go-live, there were 150 stores with 17,000 products, each with an average of 35 configurations for a total of 89,250,000 records. What's worse is that the object didn't only contain current records but also historical ones that had been overwritten during the rollout process, leading to more than 117,000,000 records in the junction object.

The object is used in a number of automations, batch jobs, and reports and is also queried frequently by custom user interface components. The design seems to have been mainly a matter of development convenience and no one seems to have ever done any calculations around the amount of data to be stored in the object.

The task force presents its conclusion and recommends a number of stopgap measures, including removing the automations, archiving all of the historical records, removing rare product configurations, tuning some reports, and implementing some caching and optimizations in the user interface.

This program of work resolves the immediate fire, but the system still doesn't perform up to expectations. Martin starts negotiations with the development partner about how to redesign the system to eliminate the root cause.

Problem

This is another anti-pattern that tends to be instigated not by an active choice but by a deprioritization of certain practices in order to deliver on a specific goal. In the case of unplanned growth, the team deprioritizes the ability to scale in order to achieve greater speed in the initial delivery.

This can be appropriate in some cases, for example, if you are a start-up trying to prove product-market fit on a shoestring budget, and for this reason, it can be subtly seductive. Many large organizations these days want to see themselves in the mold of an agile start-up, adopting many practices from this world.

However, for large well-established organizations that already have a certain scale, failing to acknowledge this fact up front is a recipe for disaster.

Proposed solution

The Unplanned Growth anti-pattern proposes that a team should get on with the important business of delivering without paying much attention to the issues that may arise due to increasing scale down the road. Effectively, the proposal is to make small-scale progress and then adapt later, should the scale be required.

This anti-pattern is different from others such as Disconnected Entities as it is not an absence of awareness that causes it, but rather an active choice to deprioritize planning for scale. Again, it is worth noting that this is not always an anti-pattern.

In some cases, starting small and then taking the hit on rework later is a justifiable strategy. Typically, this is the case if you don't know up front whether your idea will work or how many users it will need to accommodate when you are building the application partially to get more information.

But it is always an anti-pattern when done by a large organization that knows the application it is building will eventually need to reach a certain definable scale.

Results

The results of Unplanned Growth encompass a fairly large number of scaling issues, determined by the nature of the application in question. Most commonly, you will see **Large Data Volume (LDV)** type issues such as the following:

- Slowdowns in reports and dashboards
- Slowdowns in list views
- Locking issues on data loads or even in normal use
- Time-outs when loading custom components
- Errors cropping up about governor limits
- Third-party packages failing

You may also see the general UX crawl to a halt, especially if it uses many custom pages and components. Integrations can also be affected by the same issues, leading to serious errors across systems. Even automations that were working perfectly may start to fail, although not necessarily in a systematic way.

All in all, if the unplanned growth is significant enough, it can bring your entire solution to its knees.

Better solutions

The number one thing you need to do to avoid this anti-pattern is to be clear from the start about what scale you are building for. If you are planning to build something that works on a small scale to test out an idea, then that's fine, but be explicit about it and have a plan to take a step back and redesign if it turns out you are successful and need to scale.

If you know for a fact that you need to hit a certain scale, it is nearly criminal not to design for it up-front. That means incorporating LDV mitigation tactics such as the following:

- Using selective queries
- Optimizing our queries with the platform query optimizer
- Avoiding synchronous automations on LDV objects
- Avoiding synchronous code running queries on LDV objects
- Using skinny tables to optimize specific queries and reports

- Using custom indices to optimize specific queries and reports
- Archiving non-current data continuously
- Using external objects to store data externally when possible

Designing for growth also means designing the data model in a way to reduce LDV issues in the first place. In our preceding example, there would most likely be many alternative data models that did not have to hold a complete record of all product configurations by store in a single junction object.

Having now considered what happens when you fail to consider scale in the data domain, we will move on to the last anti-pattern in this chapter, which is Unconstrained Data Synchronization.

Synchronizing excessively

Data synchronization is hard to get right but extremely useful when it works. It is, however, easy to get carried away when starting to put synchronization methods in place, which can cause a plethora of problems. We'll see how in the following sections.

Unconstrained Data Synchronization

Unconstrained Data Synchronization is an anti-pattern characterized by an overly ambitious approach to synchronizing data between systems without fully appreciating all the things that can go wrong.

Example

BusyCo, a large vendor of productivity-related products, has recently implemented a B2B omnichannel digital experience spanning web, social, call center, and partner channels. They have implemented the web application using a bespoke approach based on Microsoft Azure and use Salesforce to manage any manual processing steps for quotes and orders as well as opportunity management and any quotes or orders originating via calls or field sales.

All of the information eventually goes into the **Enterprise Resource Planning (ERP)** that handles the fulfillment and financial side of the ordering process as well as serving as the source of truth for financial forecasts. Because of its role in producing financial information, the information in the ERP must always be of the highest possible quality.

Oleg, the lead architect on the Salesforce side, recommended a structured approach to data governance with clearly defined roles and responsibilities for each system in relation to the core data model objects. Also, there should be clearly defined ownership in place for key fields and objects, so the source of truth is always known.

BusyCo, however, has gone with the approach that any piece of information can be modified in any system at any point in time and all systems will be updated with the modified data in near real-time. To achieve this goal, they have put in place bidirectional data synchronization between all three systems.

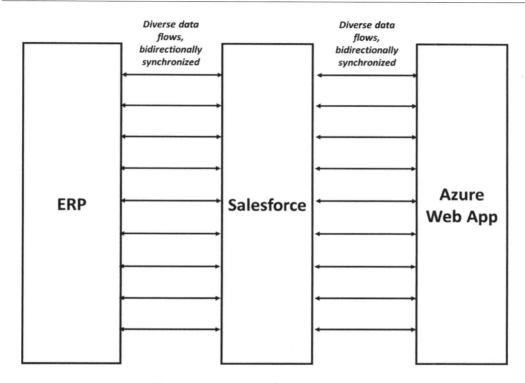

Figure 4.4 – BusyCo synchronization scenario

No problems are found during the acceptance testing phase, but Oleg is not particularly reassured. The testing scenarios do not begin to cover all of the things that can go wrong once the synchronization functions are out in the wild. The business users, however, love the flexibility of being able to change anything in whatever system context they happen to find themselves in.

After the go-live, things start to crop up. No showstoppers, but a number of annoying errors begin to emerge. One day, the link between the website and the other systems is down for a few hours and afterward a number of records fail to synchronize correctly. What's worse is that a few days later, it is discovered that some address updates were never synchronized to the ERP so some customer orders were shipped to the wrong addresses.

There is also a recurring problem with quotes that seem to go back and forth between statuses in Salesforce and the ERP. The cause seems to be a batch job running in the ERP doing some routine maintenance. As the job can't be turned off, the only solution in the short term is a manual workaround where the support team takes a daily task to reclassify quotes with a wrong status.

Moreover, there are some fringe cases around the synchronization of manually inputted quotes and orders. They don't seem to reliably trigger the data synchronization in all cases and therefore some orders hang in Salesforce and never get shipped.

As the errors compound, business leadership starts to pay more attention to voices such as Oleg's that advocate simpler patterns for managing the data between the systems. However, as the system is already live and works at least partially, any refactoring will need to be done without requiring major downtime.

Oleg accepts the challenge of finding a way to refactor the system to use simpler data integration patterns while instituting better data governance. It won't be easy, but with time and effort, he believes BusyCo can succeed.

Problem

In contrast to the last couple of anti-patterns that happened due to a lack of awareness or a failure to act, the Unconstrained Data Synchronization anti-pattern happens because of you trying your best to give the business what it wants. Sometimes, you can have the best intentions at heart and still end up causing a terrible mess.

The problem you'd be trying to solve in this case is how to have all the relevant business data available and editable in different systems at the same time. Users hate switching between contexts. If they are in System A, then they want to be able to edit all the relevant fields in System A. If they are in System B, then they want to be able to edit all the relevant fields in System B. If the fields they want to edit are the same from a master data perspective, say, an address or the name of a customer, that requirement will force you to synchronize data.

From a user experience perspective, this is perfectly rational. Switching between systems and screens in order to update data is a pain as is not having the information you need available where you need it. Equally, you usually need this information to be available in near real-time across systems to avoid processing errors.

Near real-time data synchronization can seem like a panacea, and it would be if it weren't so fiendishly complicated from a technical point of view.

Proposed solution

The solution proposed by Unconstrained Data Synchronization is to bidirectionally synchronize all relevant data points between all relevant systems in something near real-time. As noted, this can have something of a silver bullet halo attached to it and there are plenty of vendors willing to capitalize on this by promising you tools that will make synchronization easy.

The problem is that there are many failure modes in synchronization. These failures compound that the more data synchronization is used, no tool will reduce away the fundamental complexity. Small differences in processing on different systems or even within the same system can create unforeseen results, as can even minor outages or errors on some of the platforms involved. And these errors compound the more systems and objects you are synchronizing.

Unless you can confidently say you have a complete grasp of all the ways your systems and processes can fail and you are certain you have full control of all your operational processes, then Unconstrained Data Synchronization will cause you grief.

Results

Data Synchronization tends to work just fine in small-scale scenarios. Synchronizing a specific type of data between two systems is rarely a problem, so is synchronizing a relatively large amount of data unidirectionally.

The problems come when you have some combination of multiple systems, multiple objects, and bidirectional connectivity. Here, you will start to see scenarios such as those in our example where small errors compound over time to create a major problem.

Typically, what you'll get is a continuous stream of small-scale remediation activities that need to be handled by a technical support team coupled with a number of workarounds on the business level to avoid known synchronization issues. The more complex your scenario, the more of these kinds of issues you will have.

Occasionally, this anti-pattern can lead to outright disasters such as when a synchronization link fails silently for an extended period of time, leading to data between systems becoming catastrophically out of sync and business errors proliferating without anyone knowing until the complaints start coming.

Mostly, however, you just see a trickle of small issues that never seems to stop.

Better solutions

You might be expecting us to say something to the effect that you should generally avoid data synchronization. We won't. That would be naïve and unnecessary.

What we are going to say is that you should be cautious about the kinds of data synchronization you do, particularly in the following:

- Synchronizing a data point bidirectionally between two systems is fine. Don't, however, add a third.

- If you need to synchronize to more than one system, make sure that you are doing it unidirectionally and that you have defined who owns the master data.

- Middleware and synchronization tools can help with implementation, but they do not solve the fundamental problem.

- Multiple synchronizations in the same org are fine as long as they are non-overlapping; be cautious about having multiple synchronizations running for the same object.

- Synchronizations that need to run in near real-time are much more complex than those that can be processed in a batch manner.

We have now covered the anti-patterns for *Chapter 4* and are ready to move onto looking at our key takeaways for the data domain.

Knowing the takeaways

In this section, we will abstract a bit from the specific patterns and instead try to pull out the wider learning points you can use in your day-to-day work as a Salesforce architect or in preparing for the CTA Review Board.

When architecting Salesforce solutions, you should be mindful of the following:

- Salesforce has a unique approach to data modeling that does not easily map to traditional methods, such as relational database design.

- Trying to shoehorn Salesforce into such approaches will only end in tragedy.

- Instead, you should follow the good practices established by Salesforce themselves and exemplified by the data model that comes with the platform out of the box.

- This includes modeling using broad business objects rather than a normalized model, relying heavily on standard objects, and limiting the amount of custom work you put into the data layer.

- Failing to coordinate activities between teams can cause serious issues at the data model layer and really reduce your ability to get things done in future projects.

- Therefore, always promote appropriate coordination or governance forums that ensure teams understand what each one is doing.

- If possible, add to this coordination forum other data governance mechanisms such as data ownership, standards and guidance for data modeling, and approval processes for decisions that have serious data layer consequences such as adding a new custom object.

- It is a cardinal sin to know that you need to scale to a certain level and not do the necessary calculations that tell you whether that scale should be actively mitigated in your project or not.

- If you decide not to take active steps towards mitigating potential consequences of scale, you need to do so with your eyes fully open and with a plan to refactor and redesign later if needed.

- In general, failing to take scale into account can be appropriate for start-ups and experimental projects, but it is rarely appropriate in enterprise systems context.

- Business users often love the idea of data synchronization because it enables a much superior user experience. However, they rarely appreciate the technical complexities involved.

- Small-scale data synchronization is often a good way to solve a problem, but beware of scaling them too much in both size and complexity.

- Avoid synchronizing the same data points bidirectionally between more than two systems and be cautious about synchronizing large amounts of objects and fields unless it's for strictly one-way use cases, such as data going to a data warehouse.

In preparing for the CTA Review Board, you should be mindful of the following:

- Understand and follow good modeling practices when creating your data model for your scenario.

- That means modeling things the "Salesforce way" and not taking too many liberties that you'll have to explain and defend.

- Use standard objects first, and only if you are entirely convinced that no standard object will suffice should you turn to using a custom object in your solution.

- Be clear about what objects are used for what purpose and avoid having the same data in multiple places.

- Incorporate data ownership for all non-detail objects at the role level in your data model overview.

- You may want to put in a couple of words about good data governance when describing your governance model.

- Do the math on data volumes for the key objects in the scenario and clearly identify any that may have LDV requirements.

- Often these are junction objects between key entities in the system, but there are exceptions to this rule.

- Create a clear and well-thought-out LDV mitigation approach for the objects in question. Simply reciting a list of common LDV mitigation techniques is not sufficient in and of itself.

- Be careful when specifying data flows between systems. You need to be realistic in what data you propose to move back and forth and how.

- Prefer one-directional synchronizations and integrations to bidirectional ones.

- Prefer data virtualization to data synchronization whenever possible in the scenario at hand.

We have now covered the material for this chapter and are ready to proceed with the solution architecture domain. First, however, we will summarize our learning.

Summary

In this chapter, we have covered a lot of things that can go wrong in the data domain if you aren't careful. The things that go wrong in the data layer tend to affect everything in the layers above, so if you fall into any of these anti-patterns, consequences will be serious for all aspects of your future configuration, integration, and development work.

It is therefore especially important to learn the lessons of good structure, good practice, and sound governance when it comes to the data domain. Not that they are unimportant elsewhere, but if you get your data layer wrong, then it is very hard to get everything else right.

This applies both in real life and in the CTA exam. As many aspiring or current CTAs will tell you, if you get any element of your data model for a scenario substantially wrong, that tends to ripple through the other domains, making it very hard to pass the overall scenario.

Having now covered the data domain, we will proceed to solution architecture—an area so rife with anti-patterns that we'll have to be quite selective in those we choose to include.

Part 2: Solution Anti-Patterns

Part 2 will teach you how to identify and mitigate anti-patterns in the functional domain of solution architecture as well as integration architecture.

This part has the following chapters:

- *Chapter 5, Unpicking Solution Architecture Troubles*
- *Chapter 6, Keeping Integration Straight*

5

Unpicking Solution Architecture Troubles

This chapter, the longest in the book, will cover anti-patterns related to your solution architecture. We will start by looking at anti-patterns related to your choice of solutions. Then, we will look at things that can go wrong when you do functional design. Third, we will look at some particular anti-patterns that affect customizations, first at the conceptual level and then at the code level. We will end the chapter by summarizing the key takeaways.

In this chapter, we're going to cover the following main topics:

- How to avoid picking the wrong solutioning approach by basing it on bad research and analysis

- Why your assumptions can lead you astray and make your architecture and design go off the rails

- What can go wrong when you apply good features in a bad way and how to use good governance to overcome this problem

- How classic code anti-patterns also find their way into Salesforce implementations and how you can design your code with better structure and patterns

After completing this chapter, you will have a good idea about how to avoid common anti-patterns when designing solutions on Salesforce and what steps you can take to use the right solution for the right problem.

Picking the wrong thing

In this section, we will look at two anti-patterns related to picking the wrong solution based on considerations that are not technically relevant. We start by looking at what goes wrong when you ignore the wider ecosystem.

Ignoring the ecosystem

*Willfully ignoring third-party options in favor of in-house solutions can become
an anti-pattern.*

Example

SafeCo is a major insurance company that provides a variety of policies to the mass consumer market. It has a large customer service organization for which it is in the last stages of rolling out Salesforce Service Cloud to achieve a 360-degree view of customer inquiries.

Royce is a manager within SafeCo's IT department and has been tangentially related to the Service Cloud project. However, now he has been tasked with leading a team that has been asked to find good answers to a number of new generic requirements that have come up during the project but were left out of the initial scope, as outlined here:

- First, SafeCo, on learning more about Salesforce, has decided that it needs its own backup solution in place as it doesn't want to rely on the rather limited out-of-the-box offerings

- Second, while policy documents are generated by a **line-of-business** (**LOB**) system, stakeholders have identified a need for printing a number of standard letters for customers, which should be done directly from the Salesforce UI

- Finally, within the IT department, a number of people have asked whether they could have a project management tool on Salesforce as they think it would be a good platform for collaborating with business users

Royce starts by addressing the most pressing issue of backup. He's generally aware that there are a number of solutions to this problem on AppExchange, but after having a brief look, he finds them too expensive and complicated. Besides, SafeCo already has a backup infrastructure in place for other systems. Royce gets a developer in the IT department to write a script to copy Salesforce objects 1:1 to a **Structured Query Language** (**SQL**) database by exporting them to CSV files and then using a standard batch process for the import. From there, the data can be backed up using the standard SafeCo backup solution.

Document generation is another area where Royce is aware that a number of third-party solutions exist. However, there is also some internal document generation capability in the corporate **document management system** (**DMS**), and that is where he starts looking. While the solution is not perfect, the DMS team can provide the capability by accepting the request for document generation via a web service, which puts the request in a queue that is regularly emptied by a batch job that generates documents and puts them in a file share. From there, another job picks them up and uploads them back into Salesforce. It's a little slow and clunky, but it should be OK.

For the project management module, Royce has some good luck. Over a weekend, one of his team puts together a small app that seems to demonstrate a lot of the functionality SafeCo will need. He reckons that in a few weeks, he can develop something that will be good enough to roll out to the business. Royce takes the win and decides to go with it.

Royce now has his solutions, and he pushes his team hard to get them ready on time for the global service rollout. However, while nothing catastrophically fails, there are quite a few problems to contend with. The backup script works well, but when they test full and partial restores in both new and partial environments, they run into a massive and unexpected level of complexity. They abandon the **business continuity (BC)** test and make a plan to develop some more elaborate restore scripts at a later date.

As expected, there are some complaints about the slow speed of document generation, but the worse problem turns out to be template management, which Royce hadn't considered in detail during his analysis. Turns out that templates change frequently, and with the new solution, all template changes have to be done by someone in the DMS team. That makes the customer service team quite irritated.

The project management app is rolled out without major problems, but the response is underwhelming. There are a number of bugs and misunderstandings, and in general, the team was expecting to see a number of features that haven't been included. As a result, adoption across teams is lackluster.

Royce takes a breath. While everything sort of works, there are clearly a lot of issues. Royce wonders whether he might have missed something in the process, but it's time to close the project and move on.

Problem

The problem addressed in *Ignoring the ecosystem* is how to handle common capabilities related to the main requirements of implementation, but not strictly part of the core requirements. These include common backup and restore, document management and generation, automation of the deployment pipeline, the dispatch of logs to a central log server, and a range of similar requirements.

For this type of requirement (and many others to boot), there exists on Salesforce AppExchange a large number of third-party solutions that solve the particular need in a generic way, as depicted in the following screenshot. In addition, many Salesforce consulting partners have standard approaches using accelerators or internal assets that can also help with this sort of requirement:

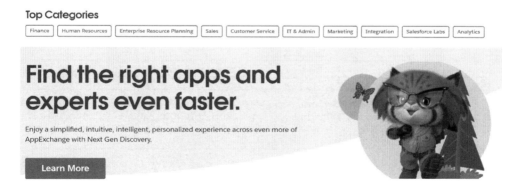

Figure 5.1 – AppExchange Top Categories section

With this anti-pattern, you ignore these options to the point of not even looking at them seriously.

Proposed solution

When you ignore the ecosystem, you actively disregard third-party options for generic requirements and instead move ahead with bespoke or in-house solutions to common capabilities. While there can be legitimate reasons for a bespoke answer to a generic requirement—for instance, if you have a highly developed infrastructure for some capability that you want to leverage across all enterprise systems—not making a reasoned comparison with the available commercial options is an anti-pattern and goes against the core philosophy of Salesforce.

That is to say, an anti-pattern arises when you do not make a considered build-versus-buy decision for important but generic capabilities and instead reflexively embrace an in-house approach, whether because of the "not invented here" syndrome or because it is cognitively easier to handle for your organization's key stakeholders.

Again, that is not to say that a build approach is never valid for these capabilities. But in my experience, you are highly likely to underestimate the complexity and ongoing costs related to these kinds of builds and will probably end up with less functionality for more money than your business case said.

Results

The results of ignoring the ecosystem are generally quite predictable, although, at the detailed level, they will obviously vary by the capability under consideration. At a higher level of abstraction, however, they tend to be as follows:

- A less capable solution that meets fewer requirements than what you could have obtained for a similar cost in the ecosystem

- Fewer new features are added to the capability over time, often at higher maintenance costs than the run-rate cost of the third-party solution

- The need to maintain an additional skillset and knowledge base for the development and maintenance of the in-house capability

- A higher degree of coupling between the new capability and the existing system than if you had used a third-party solution

- The cost picture can be complicated, but it is rare that building a generic capability yourself results in a significant saving

All in all, the results are rarely catastrophic, but commonly, the resulting solutions are worse than third-party equivalents and are achieved with greater pain and risk.

Better solutions

There is just one general piece of advice to keep in mind to avoid this anti-pattern, although implementing it can be a challenge, and that is to make a considered and well-reasoned build-versus-buy decision whenever you are encountering relatively commonplace capability requests.

To do this, you should do the following:

- Carefully explore ecosystem alternatives, both on the AppExchange and things that are available directly from your Salesforce partners.

- Engage actively with vendors; often, they are more willing to consider your unique concerns than you might think.

- Outline the potential options in enough detail to make a reasoned decision, remembering to include architectural, operational, and commercial considerations.

- Count the **Total Cost of Ownership** (**TCO**) when outlining the internal options. Often, operational, maintenance, and further development costs are undercounted in these types of comparisons.

- Drive a hard commercial bargain with third-party vendors—you can often get quite significant discounts.

Having now looked at the consequences of ignoring the ecosystem, we will now proceed to consider the consequences of fitting your solution to your licenses, rather than your licenses to your solution.

License-based solutioning

Creating a solution based on a license set that you can afford rather than the license set you really need without making the necessary compromises

Example

Alexis is the lead architect for a major Salesforce partner working directly with Salesforce on a deal for the Department of Social Welfare in the mid-sized European country, Ruritania. The department services millions of residents and has a staff of several thousand case workers spread approximately 50/50 between a central HQ and several hundred local offices. They are adopting Salesforce as a case management platform for a new high-profile initiative to help families hurt by the increasing cost of living.

As part of the deal, the Salesforce **Account Executive** (**AE**) pushed very hard for a licensing model that gave the HQ users a full Salesforce license, but only a Customer Community Plus license for the users in the local offices. He argued that as the local officers were technically members of the local municipalities, this would be acceptable under the Salesforce licensing terms and would give a more acceptable license cost for the client.

The implication, as Alexis is quick to point out, is that case workers will be working in two different interfaces, one internal and one external, based on a community. However, the AE argues that the differences are minor and that most of the work done for the internal interface can be replicated directly in the community.

While that is generally true, as work continues, many subtle differences start to make an impact. There are differences in what Customer Community Plus users can have access to within the system and also differences in which things can be exposed on a Lightning page versus a Community page and how this can be done.

This situation forces increasing amounts of functionality into custom code, especially into a collection of small **Lightning Web Components (LWCs)** to accommodate the two interfaces. Furthermore, all test cases need to be written and executed twice, once for each interface, adding considerable overhead.

When it comes to rolling out the application, they also need to create two versions of the documentation, the training materials, and the actual user training. Alexis also flags that her company will need to increase the application maintenance fee as there is a lot more customization to maintain and many future changes will need to be done in two versions.

The users are generally happy with the new application, but there are a lot of communication errors and mistakes caused by the differences in the interface between the local offices and the HQ. The financial director within the Department of Social Welfare is also unhappy with the increase in implementation cost and application maintenance he has seen, which he does not feel are fully compensated by the lower license cost.

Problem

The problem addressed by license-based solutioning is an old chestnut. How do we deliver all the required functionality within the cost envelope we've been given? If you've never had to struggle with fitting user demands to a budget that is just too small for the level of ambition, I want to know where you work so I can apply.

It is nearly universally true that stakeholders would like more features than they have money to buy. One way to try to get around this is to try to carefully optimize the licenses you buy in order to get the best value for money. This is called license optimization and is an essential skillset on the Salesforce platform. You can see an overview of the Salesforce license model in the following diagram:

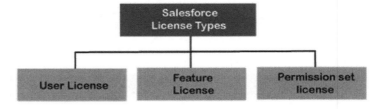

Figure 5.2 – Salesforce license model

License-based solutioning turns this commendable practice into an anti-pattern by specifying first which licenses can be afforded and then shoehorning the rest of the solution to make it fit.

Proposed solution

License-based solutioning proposes to make an affordable license mix work for a given set of requirements by using workarounds and custom functionality to fill the gap between the actually required license type and the license type you can afford. That is to say, you engage in this anti-pattern when there is a standard license type that would meet the user requirements, but you instead choose to go with a bespoke or partially bespoke solution that somehow bridges the functionality that is available in the license you have and the license you would really want.

A few common examples include the following:

- Using community licenses for users that are for all intents and purposes internal—although just external enough for there not to be a blatant breach of terms—who ideally would use the internal UI if it were not too expensive

- Using shadow objects to replicate standard objects that are not covered by your license type—for instance, having a shadow case object bi-directionally replicating the information from Case to allow internal case workers to have a cheaper platform license

- Replicating key features from industry clouds—for example, Action Plans—because of an unwillingness to adopt additional licenses

- License sharing between different users that have the same organizational role, circumventing terms and security

- Using cheaper solutions for some features—for example, using a WordPress site instead of a community to save license costs and then syncing the data between the site and Salesforce

While there can be a commercial rationale for these practices, from a technical perspective, they are undoubtedly maladaptive.

Results

The results can vary depending on the specific use case, but often they include things like the following:

- Increased need for custom work to compensate for the lack of license features

- Overall increased complexity of the solution in order to make the different parts fit together in a reasonable way

- More maintenance going forward as a result of the increased custom work and increased overall complexity

- Reduction in value from future feature upgrades as you will need to consider the added customization work

- Reduced security from license sharing or reusing a single license for many functions

This can leave you in a gray area vis-à-vis Salesforce as the licensing agreement is not easy for laypeople to interpret and Salesforce is not transparent about how it enforces the terms in cases where there is considerable ambiguity.

That being said, from a TCO perspective, it is sometimes true that you might be better off not buying the licenses and doing custom work instead. Salesforce licenses are expensive, and if you only need a little bit of what's included in a feature license, you may be able to rebuild it for a lower price.

However, my advice would be to avoid this if at all possible and instead seek an alternative option, as we'll discuss in the next section.

Better solutions

In general, you are better off trying to negotiate a better deal with Salesforce, looking at third-party options for the specific functionality you need, or reengineering the solution to avoid the specific features you need either by changing the scope or redefining who needs which feature license.

Let's look at these in turn:

1. Your first port of call, when faced with unaffordable licenses, should be to push your Salesforce AE harder. They often have considerable leeway to offer discounts, especially if we're talking about a new license type or you are willing to commit to a longer time period for the deal. It also helps to push shortly before the end of Salesforce's financial quarters.

2. Second, you should look at third-party options. You can look at AppExchange to see if a less expensive product might meet your needs, or you can ask your implementation partners if they have assets you might be able to leverage.

3. Third, you can go back to the business and ask them to reprioritize features so that you can either cut something else to make space for the licensing cost or remove features that require the extra license.

4. Fourth, you can go back and do another round of license optimization where you go through the detail of the proposed licensing and see where you can cut specific licenses for specific users. Often, some licenses are must-haves for some users, but only nice to haves for others.

If you can't find a good solution and have to go ahead with this anti-pattern, be sure to do so with an awareness of the real cost and risk involved. That being said, we will now proceed to our next anti-pattern, *assumption-driven customization*.

Applying the thing wrong

In this section, we will consider two anti-patterns where we get unsatisfactory solutions based on a failure of the assumptions we bring to the table. These assumptions can be either about user needs or the capabilities of our technology—both can lead to trouble.

Assumption-driven customization

Letting the assumptions of a small, unrepresentative group stand in for the needs of the wider user base

Example

Helene is the product owner for a new initiative to roll out Health Cloud within LifeCo, a major provider of medical devices for monitoring certain chronic diseases. In addition to the Health Cloud rollout, LifeCo is also developing a custom care application that will be used by **healthcare professionals (HCPs)**, principally nurses, working in clinics associated with LifeCo's care programs.

Helene was a nurse for several years before entering the IT field after working as a **subject-matter expert (SME)** on a few major IT products. Therefore, she feels that she has a strong grasp of the requirements and also has several friends, still working as nurses, who she uses as sounding boards.

After some internal discussions, Helene has decided to deliver the application as an app optimized for the kinds of tablet computers she knows are common within clinics. That will allow HCPs to directly note down information relevant to the care programs as they are interacting with patients.

The team develops an attractive and highly functional tablet application that meets all of the key requirements Helene has identified. In initial user testing with a friendly audience, the app receives great praise, and everyone is looking forward to the production rollout.

However, as they are starting to plan the rollout, many clinics push back and refuse to implement the new application. After digging into the issue, it turns out that staff in many clinics, while they have tablet devices available, prefer not to use them directly with patients as they feel it hampers the interaction.

For other HCPs, the idea of capturing the data directly while with the patient goes against a longstanding practice of collecting information in paper notes during the course of the day and then typing it into the system after hours, using a PC with an interface highly optimized for rapid data entry. The HCPs feel that switching to the new system would force them to spend more time on data entry and decrease the impact of patient contact.

Helene has a long list of counterarguments to address the concerns raised by the HCPs and strongly feels that with a modicum of training and process change, the end users will come to see how the new application can significantly improve their working practices. However, she is met with the unfortunate fact that none of the clinics refusing to adopt the new application is owned directly by LifeCo, so there is no way to force them to change.

This presents a major issue to LifeCo as that means they have to keep the old system for managing care programs live and that they will have two separate databases of care information used at the same time, causing serious consolidation issues. Helene is pushed to find a quick solution that will satisfy the hold-out clinics.

In the end, she has to relent. She sits down with her team to see what can be done to create a version of the app that can be used from a PC. They quickly port the key functionality and release a barebones version to the clinics that have declined to accept the tablet application. While it gets a lukewarm response, at least this time no one refuses to use it.

Problem

The thing with assumption-driven customization is that it's less about the problem it's trying to solve—that could theoretically be anything—and more about the way you are trying to solve it. With assumption-driven customization, you are trying to solve a problem as defined by your product management, product owners, or developers.

Only, it turns out that the actual problem you need to solve was something else entirely. The problem with assumption-driven customization, in other words, is that you are unwittingly trying to solve the wrong problem.

This is different from just getting the requirements wrong because it can happen with good teams following a good process. All it takes is for the sample that you are using to represent your user base to be in some way systematically biased, as we saw in our example.

Proposed solution

The proposed solution of assumption-driven customization is to let a group of experts stand in for the wider user base in order to facilitate rapid delivery of the solution being built. This is a perfectly reasonable approach. We let experts guide us in most things, and generally, it works quite well.

This only goes wrong if, for some reason, your representative experts turn out to have systematic biases relative to your real user base—for instance, someone who used to work in a function but now is out of touch with day-to-day reality or someone who has made the transition to an IT career some time ago and has now adopted an IT perspective on things.

Note that sometimes you want to roll something out that is not what your user base wanted or expected in order to drive transformational change. That is a different ballgame and is all about the way you do change management. However, if you do it unintentionally and unknowingly, you have an anti-pattern.

Results

Basically, the results of assumption-driven customization depend on the degree of misfit with user needs and expectations:

- At one end of the scale, you have a set of basically benign misunderstandings that can be fixed with goodwill, training, and a set of workarounds.

- If that is insufficient, you may have to add or rework a limited number of features in order to get the users to a place where they are happy to work with the new system. This is still relatively manageable.

- However, sometimes you get to a point where users flat-out refuse to adopt a new system, even with substantial modifications.

- At this point, you have two options: either you force it through and deal with the backlash from the user base or you scrap the tool and go back to the old way of doing things.

The following diagram provides a visual representation of the scale of results:

Figure 5.3 – Scale of deteriorating results for assumption-driven customization

That is to say, the consequences of this anti-pattern, while often minor, can be disastrous, and you should spend time being mindful about avoiding it.

Better solutions

This is a difficult pattern to guard against because it occurs when the people we trust to be the voice of our user base fail in some significant ways to represent those users. It can be deeply uncomfortable having to raise these kinds of issues with Product Managers or Product Owners who are convinced about their own position, and in fairness, most of the time they will be right.

However, there are some mechanisms that can help with this:

- Broader consultation with the user base—for instance, via larger events or a common online forum.

- Earlier feedback from the broader user base. Roadshows, demo videos, and webinars are good options here.

- Sprint-by-spring acceptance testing from a larger user group.

- If you are looking to create deep change, plan for it, and include the necessary change management. Never try to sneak in a major change.

That concludes our discussion of this anti-pattern. We will now move on to a genuine classic: the Golden Hammer.

The Golden Hammer

The Golden Hammer makes the fundamental error of mistaking a tool that is a good solution for some use cases for a tool that is a good solution for all use cases.

Example

WheelCo is a large manufacturer of tires, especially for the transportation sector. It is rolling out Salesforce with Manufacturing Cloud at its core to closely connect its manufacturing and sales processes.

As part of the deal it has made with Salesforce, WheelCo has received unlimited use of OmniStudio and has been party to a number of pieces of training and accelerators related to the capabilities of the product. As a result, the architects, developers, and business users within WheelCo are extremely excited about what OmniStudio can do for their business.

During initial architecture discussions, the decision is made to base the entire solution on the OmniStudio toolset, including all UI processes (both internal and external), integrations, and any subsidiary processes where OmniStudio could conceivably be used. Only batch and asynchronous processes are left out of scope. That way, WheelCo believes it will maximize the value it can generate from the Salesforce purchase.

The project starts, and in many areas, rapid progress is made. To stay consistent, most parts of the standard UI are ignored and FlexCards and OmniScripts instead make up nearly the entire **user experience (UX)**. Integrations are developed using integration procedures, except for a few that run in the background.

The volume of development is much larger than originally anticipated, but by adding a sufficient amount of resources, WheelCo still manages to get its implementation done on time. It has some trouble finding enough qualified resources that have the required level of OmniStudio experience, but by paying top rates, it manages to secure enough people for the project to succeed.

The go-live is, broadly speaking, successful, although there is some grumbling that not everything that was promised has made it into the release. A number of key features had to be descoped during development to make it on time.

Over the following year, some problems with the solution start to become evident. The integrations are not as flexible as was expected and cannot accommodate all the different use cases the business wants to add. There is also a problem with new feature releases on the Salesforce platform. Every time something new is added, it takes a change to OmniScripts, FlexCards, and sometimes supporting code to make it available to users.

The cost of supporting the solution is also high. Basically, any change needs intervention from a senior technical person, and that reduces the flexibility of the platform. Within WheelCo, many start to question whether OmniStudio really was the right solution to all the requirements it was used for in the project.

This is especially true as some of the native Manufacturing Cloud features that were excluded from the OmniStudio work seem to be rapidly improving without anyone needing to lift a finger to make it work.

After about a year, WheelCo's CTO appoints a new Chief Architect, who has as one of his early priorities to look at the architecture of the Salesforce platform. He identifies high complexity caused by large amounts of customization as a major driver of cost and functional issues. To address the issue, he recommends refactoring the solution to use a much more standardized UI, retaining OmniStudio for complex multi-step processes and areas where particular views of the data and associated actions generate real value and eliminating it elsewhere.

Problem

The Golden Hammer solves any problems—that is the nature of the Golden Hammer. Once you have found the Golden Hammer, every problem you encounter is a fit. There is no evaluation of fitness for purpose because the Golden Hammer is obviously the right solution.

The tech industry, in general, is very prone to Golden Hammers. We are always looking for the next cool technology to solve our problems. Salesforce with its aggressive sales approach and Kool-Aid drinking community is perhaps even more prone to this anti-pattern than most platforms in the technology space.

Note that Golden Hammers are often technically excellent solutions within their own solution space, but they are stretched well beyond that space because of enthusiasm, hype, and excitement.

Proposed solution

The solution proposed by the Golden Hammer is the Golden Hammer. That is to say, whatever the problem, whatever the parameters of the problem, they will somehow be twisted into something the Golden Hammer could conceivably deliver, or alternately, the Golden Hammer will be twisted into something that delivers a solution to the problem.

If you have to pick, it's better to mold the problem to a bad-fitting tool than to use a tool for a problem that it is definitely unsuitable for. However, it goes without saying that neither of these options is particularly good.

A good way to check if you are under the influence of a Golden Hammer is to notice whether your discussions about new technology features start with looking for problems your tech stack could deliver or whether you start with problems and then try to find a suitable technology stack. If it's the first, you need to be careful as you could have a Golden Hammer on your hands.

Results

The results of a Golden Hammer depend on the degree of technical badness of fit that you have engaged in:

- At a minimum, you will end up with a gap versus the requirements that you were meant to fulfill as there will be areas the Golden Hammer didn't really manage to solve because it's not the thing it was meant to solve

- Higher cost and more customization work as you increasingly stretch the Golden Hammer beyond its capabilities

- Additional maintenance work and resulting cost as a result of the overstretched solution that has been created

- Reduced faith in the real capabilities of the Golden Hammer within the organization, even where it is genuinely a good fit

- A need to maintain a specialist skillset across different areas in your business that will persist even when the hammer is no longer popular or trending

All in all, the results will depend on how much you are stretching the tool's capabilities, but choosing the tool before you know the problem is invariably an anti-pattern.

Better solutions

Architects differ in their willingness to adopt new tools and technologies. Salesforce architects, in my experience, are fairly aggressive in adopting new technologies as long as they are on the platform. I am therefore probably going to come off as a bit of a curmudgeon when I say that my general recommendation is to be quite conservative about adopting the newest toolsets, especially on Salesforce.

In the Salesforce ecosystem, we are constantly bombarded with new features, new toolsets, and new ways of doing things. While that is great, changing an approach that has worked for you in the past and that continues to deliver value to your organization should only be done after careful consideration and definitely not because Salesforce has just launched a shiny new toy.

Instead, take a gradual, incremental approach where you try out new toolsets of smaller features and projects that do not have a business-critical impact. Don't just do prototypes or **proofs of concept** (**POCs**) as these are easy to get right but use them for real but limited business use cases. Get the learnings, then scale it across your estate if it genuinely delivers value. If it doesn't deliver value to your organization, leave it alone, even if it's very cool.

Engineering overflow

The two anti-patterns in this section both represent failures of technical governance, resulting from too much engineered work going into a single component without appropriate design patterns and practices applied to mitigate it.

Automation bonanza

Automation bonanza is what happens when you fail to govern how automations are used on your key objects.

Example

DrinksCo is a long-time user of the Salesforce platform, using it for sales and customer service as well as having a large and elaborate footprint on Marketing Cloud. While there are multiple orgs in use across the estate, there is one main org that manages the core processes for which Salesforce is in use.

While this org has been creaking slightly for a while, the situation has now gotten to a point where DrinksCo users are making serious complaints. The time to save records on key objects such as Opportunity and Account can sometimes be measured in minutes. Occasionally, records will simply fail to save, giving an obscure technical error message. Worse still, there are synchronization jobs containing important information about new leads and opportunities that randomly fail without giving a clear explanation as to why.

Francesca is a Salesforce consultant with a boutique Salesforce partner. She is called in to analyze the situation and propose improvements to the org that ideally fix the root cause of the issues, but at the minimum reduce the symptoms quickly.

After a week of examining the org, she is no longer in doubt. The problems are caused by interaction effects between a large number of complex automations on key objects. On Opportunity, for instance, there are deep layers of automation that evolved over many years that combine to create serious issues.

This includes a large and complex Apex trigger, two additional triggers from managed packages, a handful of workflow rules, three process builders, yet to be migrated to flows, a before-record-triggered flow, an after-record-triggered flow, several batch jobs that operate on the object, and multiple integrations directly using both the native API and a custom web service to manipulate records in the Opportunity object.

Francesca takes a deep breath and starts methodically mapping out the various sequences of events that can occur depending on the Opportunity records and their updates. She does this by systematically following the order of execution and looking at where there might be potential undesirable interaction effects between the different automations.

After some time, she concludes that the number of ways in which it is possible for these sequences to go wrong is too high for the current model to stand. It is unfixable without seriously reducing the complexity of the automations.

Therefore, she devises a refactoring plan that she believes will be successful in alleviating the most serious symptoms of the Opportunity object, although probably not entirely eliminating the problem. If it is successful for the Opportunity object, similar initiatives will be attempted for other key objects in the core org.

The plan includes moving the process builders and several of the workflow rules into the two flows, consolidating the integrations so that there is only one that regularly handles imports into Opportunity, simplifying the Apex trigger, and getting rid of one of the managed packages that aren't strictly needed anymore.

The plan takes much longer than initially expected to implement—there are just too many things to consider for everything to go to plan. But eventually, the users start reporting an improved experience when using Opportunity. The old random errors no longer occur. And although saving is still slower than they would like, it is no longer so slow as to be a serious issue.

Having momentarily enjoyed her success, Francesca takes another deep breath and starts the process for the other key objects in the org.

Problem

The problem that automation bonanza tries to resolve is how to accommodate different architectural styles or preferences when creating automations on Salesforce. That occurs almost inevitably when you have multiple teams working on the same objects as part of different projects and often coming from different implementation partners.

There are many ways to automate business processes in Salesforce, and different teams will have different takes on the best way for their particular requirements. That is fine if you have just one team working on its own objects, but gets messy when you have more.

That's when you need a way to guide the evolution of your architecture over time to keep things consistent. If you fail to do so, you may end up with automation bonanza.

Proposed solution

Automation bonanza responds to the multiplicity of automation options, some of which are shown in the following screenshot, and the commensurate multiplicity of automation approaches by allowing for diversity. That is to say, teams are allowed to choose a best-fit approach in isolation:

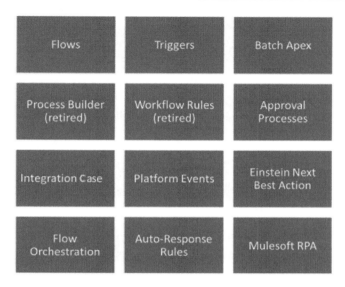

Figure 5.4 – Some Salesforce automation options

This reduces coordination requirements between the teams and usually doesn't result in short-term issues. Therefore, it can be quite difficult to spot that you have a problem or are generating a problem before things have already gone wrong.

Results

The negative consequences of automation bonanza can be rich and varied. Some of the things that frequently occur are included next:

- Slowing performance on key record pages—sometimes, saves can take a long time to complete
- Failures in integration call-ins, especially where these update records in batches or in a bulk fashion
- Failures in batch jobs or import jobs
- Strange, unpredictable errors occurring in the UI, typically associated with a save or update event
- Difficulties in debugging issues occurring on the platform as interaction effects from automations overshadow the general picture

Overall, if you get into a serious case of automation bonanza, you can have a real mess on your hands. What's worse is that this tends to happen first to your most treasured objects as these are the ones used the most across projects.

Better solutions

The key to avoiding the automation bonanza anti-pattern is good architecture governance around your core objects and their automations. Some things to keep in mind in order to do this include the following:

- You should start by defining which types of automation you want to use in your org and for which use cases.

- Ideally, you want a number as close to one as possible for each object. Choose either flows or triggers as your go-to automation type and stick to it.

- It is possible to mix Apex and flows safely, but it requires careful planning and a good framework.

- If using flows as your principal mechanism, make callouts to Apex via Actions rather than by creating triggers unless forced to do so for performance reasons.

- Also, be sure to have a framework that helps the architect use flows. This should include the use of sub-flows to keep flexibility. Have decoupled automation processes that are easy to troubleshoot in case of problems instead of having a large monolithic flow containing all the business logic in a tightly coupled design that in the long term is complex and expensive to maintain.

- If using triggers as your principal mechanism, use a trigger framework such as Apex Trigger Actions (`https://github.com/mitchspano/apex-trigger-actions-framework`), which enables you to call out to flows as part of the trigger execution.

- Avoid Process Builders and workflow rules as these are being retired.

- Batch processes and incoming integrations need to be designed carefully and mindful of existing automations. Remember mechanisms such as bypass flags that enable you to selectively bypass automations for some processes.

- Watch managed package triggers and flows carefully. You don't have control over them, but they may still cause trouble by interacting with your own functionality.

In general, trying to keep your automation approach simple and uniform will generate substantial long-term benefits for your Salesforce orgs. That being said, we will now proceed to the next anti-pattern: overweight component.

Overweight component

An overweight component is a single component that has grown into an application of its own without having the architecture and design to sustain it.

Example

HealthyMindCo is a broker for mental health services across the United Kingdom. It is implementing a new case management solution on Salesforce. In this solution, case workers collect relevant information about new clients and determine which actual local provider is best placed to help them. Additionally, they track the consultations their clients go through in order to determine the effectiveness of the intervention.

The company has very special requirements around the recommendations the system should make for potential treatment options and referral possibilities, which can only really be accommodated by using a custom code. Because HealthyMindCo prefers a simple and highly optimized UX, Amir, the project lead for the partner implementing the solution, decides to go with a Lightning component that can incorporate the necessary logic for creating new cases.

Initially, the thought is that the component will only be used for new cases. However, after initial user testing, it is clear that update functionality will also need to be added. There are too many instances where initial assumptions need to be checked, which can lead to different outcomes in terms of the treatment plan.

After the update functionality has been added, the component is tested with users again, and what appears to be evident is that the component will also need to support the management of activities and activity templates as that is a crucial part of the initial setup of a treatment plan. The team works hard to add this to the component, which is starting to be a substantial piece of engineering.

Once the activities and activity templates have been added to the component, a number of users point out that it doesn't make any sense to have the activity management part of the equation in the new component, which is now coming to be known simply as the case-handling component, and also not to have the tracking of SLAs against those activities in the component. This implies also adding the visit-tracking capability as that is required to manage the SLAs.

At this point, the Lightning component is the main interface used by HealthyMindCo staffers. As that is the case, a number of integration callouts that get information from other systems are added directly to the code in the component, simply because this is where it will be used anyways.

The system goes live in an unspectacular manner. There are a lot of bugs, in particular in the case-handling component. But with a lot of goodwill and hard work, the team comes to a level where the quality is just acceptable enough for the client to use it in anger.

After the go-live, HealthyMindCo keeps finding new bugs in the case-handling interface. It is generally quite unstable. In addition, it still wants to add large amounts of new functionality to it. However, the company is not happy with the quotes it is receiving for its change requests.

Amir consults with some of the senior architects within his company. They assess the situation and tell him that the component is too big, too monolithic, and too difficult to maintain. He needs to refactor the code base and find the funding to do so either from the client or internally. He tries, but no one seems particularly inclined to pick up the tab.

Problem

Generally, heavyweight components are built to accommodate a real or perceived need for a custom UX that goes well beyond what can be delivered with Salesforce's out-of-the-box tools. Note that in some cases, the perception that you need such a specialized UX can be stronger than reality.

Users that come from old systems that have been used to working in a specialized application or who had their old system customized heavily to their needs might assume that such customization will also be necessary on a platform such as Salesforce. There can be a marked degree of skepticism in some users toward the idea of using standard functionality. We all like to think that what we do is somehow special, after all.

Not to say that there aren't cases where there is a genuine need to have a unique and highly customized UX but, in my experience, they are less common than many would think. In any case, the way a heavyweight component attempts to deliver such an experience is less than ideal.

Proposed solution

A heavyweight component proposes to deliver a unique UX within Salesforce, using a development framework such as LWC to create what is effectively an embedded monolith application residing on the platform. This can be attractive for a number of reasons:

- You have full control of the UX and UI within a single component, allowing you to respond to almost any user request

- All functions are integrated, and the architecture is simple to understand

- There is one place for everything, and all changes can be made there, reducing the need for tooling and coordination

- The component is still embedded within the standard UX and with judicious use of styling may even look like something that came as standard

- You can accommodate changes to the UX within the component, giving users more of what they need

This solution also tends to not seem dangerous at the outset, even to experienced architects and developers, because all we're talking about is "just" another LWC component. It's only when the true scope of that component is realized that it becomes a problem.

Results

While the component remains relatively small, you will not see any negative results, and, of course, lightweight components are useful and architecturally appropriate elements of most Salesforce architectures. However, as a component grows and grows, it starts to resemble a standalone application, a code-based monolith that lives within the larger application but still has a life of its own.

Often, this happens unintentionally when a component that was meant to do something relatively simple evolves into a catch-all location for functionality. In fact, this often happens because the initial component was very successful, and users want it to do more things.

The consequences of this evolution are familiar:

- Quality starts to decrease and the error rate increases as the new component grows too big and complex for developers to handle

- Maintenance slows down, and bug fixes and feature requests take longer to come through the pipeline

- Only certain developers can work on the heavyweight component because it gets too complex for others to handle

- The overall UX begins to deteriorate due to the reduced quality and crowded functionality

- The component is increasingly hard to integrate with other parts of the platform and is increasingly treated as a standalone application

Occasionally, this pattern can deteriorate to such an extent that you end up with a Big Ball of Mud—see *Chapter 2*. However, even when it doesn't go that far, you will eventually need a major refactoring effort to address the issues.

Better solutions

Given that the issue with a heavyweight component is that you effectively end up with a monolith application without a well-defined architecture, it shouldn't be a surprise that the way to address the anti-pattern is to improve the architecture of the custom functionality you are going to deliver.

Generally, this is done by decomposing the larger component into a set of smaller more manageable pieces, while leveraging as much standard functionality as you can. Using an **event-driven architecture** (**EDA**) that allows the smaller components to communicate by sending and responding to events can also be helpful.

Additionally, architecture governance has a key role to play in this anti-pattern. You should have an assessment and approval process in place for new components, and you should also have someone periodically check in on what happens with the custom components that get approved as they can tend to balloon.

That doesn't mean you need a formal code audit to check through what everyone is doing unless your project is very large, but you should have architects that are part of your governance approach and who know the detail of what is going on with any custom development done in your org. That will help you spot evolving issues early.

Now, we will move on to our two code-focused anti-patterns, starting with the God class.

Making a mess of code

The last two anti-patterns of the chapter are focused on two anti-patterns that happen in code. While these aren't the most common in the Salesforce world, we as architects should still be aware that our code-based solutions must adhere to good practice or fall into common anti-patterns.

God class

The God class is a single class that contains all or most of the business logic defined for an application.

Example

ShoeCo, a maker of some of the world's most popular sneaker brands, has a complex, multi-cloud Salesforce org that it uses to run key parts of its business. As it has many custom requirements as well as a substantial amount of legacy on the platform, it has a large number of Apex classes to handle both business logic and integrations.

It has recently started to make the switch to flows, and in practice, most functionality is a combination of code and declarative functionality. Over time, ShoeCo would like to simplify its Salesforce functionality and avoid some of the problems it is currently facing.

In particular, many of the architects at ShoeCo are starting to feel like the org is out of control and that they don't have any clear overview of the logic that is activated at different parts of the system. Pranit, one of the Salesforce architects, makes a proposal to simplify the current system architecture by creating a `CentralDispatch` Apex class that will take the role of dispatching calls to other code or flows.

With all business logic funneled through the `CentralDispatch` class, Pranit believes that it will be much easier to identify which code is called in which circumstances, allowing for greater transparency, lower maintenance costs, and a greater potential for code reuse.

A key philosophical requirement for this approach is that the `CentralDispatch` class should contain no logic of its own. It is just there to forward requests to the right handler. However, this philosophical principle is soon abrogated in practice.

In order to make the class work as intended, more and more of the business logic that determines what gets called in which contexts has to move into the `CentralDispatch` class itself. That means more and more of the actual functionality lives in a class that is growing ever larger by the day.

While this causes some concern initially, Pranit and his fellow architects accept the development as they still have better visibility than before the introduction of the `CentralDispatch` class. It is only when developers start to complain that the class is too big and can't be changed without there being unknown side effects in various parts of the system that they start to take serious notice.

The class has grown to more than 5,000 lines of Apex code, and it effectively orchestrates all logic called from other places within the ShoeCo org. To some extent, it has been a victim of its own success, but at this point, most of the developers consider it more of a hindrance than a boon.

Pranit decides to create a new plan to refactor the `CentralDispatch` class and get it back to its original skinny self. He wants to move out all the complex logic and keep it as a dispatch hub that determines which other Apex code or flows get called in particular contexts.

However, on inspecting the code, he finds that actually, it is in many cases impossible to do that kind of request forwarding without also including substantial amounts of logic. Disheartened, he considers whether the approach needs to be fundamentally changed.

Problem

The God class anti-pattern is deployed to centralize technical problem-solving with an application. Basically, it can be much easier, conceptually speaking, to use a single pattern deployed in a single class to manage all the technical complexity that arises during custom development than to spend a lot of time doing detailed architecture and design.

You can see the God class code structure in the following diagram:

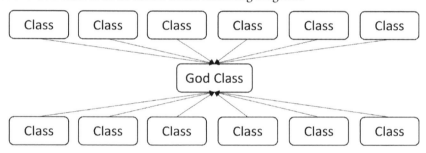

Figure 5.5 – God class code structure

You don't see this anti-pattern frequently in Salesforce implementations, but it is a real danger to ISVs building for AppExchange or any organization building bespoke apps on the Salesforce platform.

Proposed solution

The God class is a single file, generally an Apex class when we are talking about Salesforce, that hosts all or at least the majority of the critical business logic of a complex application. Centralizing functionality in this way can seem like a good design decision as it makes the overall architecture and design quite manageable, and there are even some patterns, such as the Dispatcher pattern used in our preceding example, that can be quite effectively used in such a centralized way.

Often as an application evolves, you can start to lose the big picture. This is especially true if you have a small application that is growing into a big application over time. You probably didn't have a strong architecture in mind at the outset as it was only meant to be a small app that could be built quickly.

In this case, resorting to centralization of the code base can be a way of managing the application and getting back in control. Or, you might simply have started to put all the logic in one place for convenience and you didn't really notice that the class had grown to several thousand lines of code.

However, as with all cases of poorly managed evolution of functionality, you will end up paying the costs eventually.

Results

At this point in the book, you should be able to predict the negative outcomes from an anti-pattern that results from badly managed application growth. We have seen a number of such patterns, from heavyweight component to Big Ball of Mud, and indeed the God class shares many of the negative consequences we have come to expect:

- The code gets hard to understand, resulting in longer maintenance cycles, slower new development, and increased error rates

- Only certain programmers may be able to work on the God class to avoid unfortunate side effects

- All changes in the code base, anywhere, also require changes to the God class

- There are often strange interaction effects between what happens in the God class and what happens in the rest of the system, leading to hard-to-debug errors

- The class presents a **single point of failure** (SPOF) within the application, and if it fails, none of the additional logic can be processed

Overall, you end up with an application that is fragile, brittle, and a bit of a mess.

Better solutions

When building custom solutions on Salesforce, you will generally be using Apex, an **object-oriented** (**OO**) language closely related to Java. That means you should be following good **OO analysis and design (OOAD)** practices if you are proposing to build anything non-trivial on the platform. While teaching OOAD is way beyond the scope of this book, a good place to start is by studying the SOLID principles.

The **SOLID** principles are a set of guidelines that can be used when designing software to make it more understandable, maintainable, and extensible. The acronym stands for **Single responsibility**, **Open-closed**, **Liskov substitution**, **Interface segregation**, and **Dependency injection (DI)**. These are described briefly here:

- The **Single Responsibility Principle (SRP)** is the principle that a class or module should have one, and only one, reason to change. This principle is often used in conjunction with the **Open-Closed Principle (OCP)**.

- The OCP states that software should be open for extension but closed for modification. This means that new functionality should be added by extending the existing code, rather than modifying it.

- Liskov substitution is a principle in **OO programming** (**OOP**) that states that objects of a superclass should be able to be replaced with objects of its subclasses without changing the functionality of the program.

- Interface segregation is the process of separating a single interface into multiple, smaller interfaces. This can be done for a variety of reasons, such as increasing the modularity of a system or reducing the complexity of an interface.

- DI is a technique for achieving loose coupling between objects and their dependencies. It involves providing a component with its dependencies, rather than allowing it to create or obtain them itself. This can be done either manually by the programmer or automatically by a tool.

Having now covered the God class, we will move on to our last pattern of the chapter: error hiding.

Error hiding

Error hiding is what happens when you hide technical errors from end users
without adopting a structured error-handling approach.

Example

SailCo, a provider of custom-designed sailboats, has a complex configuration app for configuring the boats it sells, which it has built on top of the Salesforce platform. The app is built in a fairly traditional way using a combination of LWCs and Apex code.

SailCo users are in general extremely non-technical, and one of the key requirements that the custom app had to satisfy was to never show a technical error message to an end user. Therefore, the developers of the original application devised a way to catch all exceptions and wrap them in a generic error message before being shown to the user.

This general message telling users that an error has occurred in a friendly way is the main error message seen in the system, as the developers were unable or didn't have sufficient time to differentiate the errors that might occur in a reasonable way. Users, however, seem comfortable enough with the solution and don't enquire much about the exact nature of the errors that occasionally occur.

However, after a while, it becomes clear that there are some systematic ways in which the configuration app can fail. In fact, there are complaints from several customers that their desired configurations have not been successfully captured as part of the order they have made and that had been registered in Salesforce using the custom app.

No one can pinpoint the error exactly, and it falls to Sarah, a relatively junior Salesforce engineer, to try to debug the problem. She starts by reviewing the logs that she can generate from the production system but finds that the only errors she can see are the generic error messages thrown by the wrapping mechanism that hides the technical information from the users. In many cases, exceptions are simply caught but never handled.

That means the production logs are, effectively, of no use to her debugging efforts. She tries to reproduce the errors in lower environments after making some changes to the code to get the raw stack trace instead of the wrapped error message. However, she is unable to reproduce the errors in the lower environments.

She seeks and eventually gets permission for a special production release to add improved logging to the system. However, she needs to do a major refactoring of the existing code base as the quick hack she had used initially was not deemed fit for production use.

After having done the major code refactor with the help of a few other SailCo developers, she manages to get the new logging functionality into production. As luck would have it, the problem turns out to be a trivial coding error.

Sarah fixes the issue and releases the new code to production, confident that with the new error-handling approach, she will be able to find issues even if the current fix doesn't address all the problems that may be found in the code base.

Problem

Error hiding is done for an excellent reason: not showing end users ugly technical error messages that are going to confuse them and make them lose faith in our application. In an ideal world, we want to recover gracefully from all errors or at least show a friendly, easy-to-understand error message.

You can see a simple example of error hiding here:

```
public class OpportunityAddController {
        public Opportunity newOpp {get; set;}

        public OpportunityAddController(){
                newOpp = new Opportunity();
        }

        public void addOpp(){
                try{
                        insert newOpp;
                }
                catch(Exception ex){ }
        }
}
```

Figure 5.6 – Simple example of error hiding

In practice, we mostly only have time to analyze the most common failure modes during analysis and design, leaving a large number of potential failures that we have not prepared for. With the error hiding anti-pattern, we end up hiding all of these errors not only from the end user but also from ourselves.

Proposed solution

The error hiding anti-pattern solves the problem of not showing end users technical error messages by simply hiding away errors or replacing any error with a generic innocuous error message. This is done technically in a way where an exception is caught and the information contained in that exception is simply discarded, whether or not a message is shown to the end user.

That means we have no logging or systematic capture of error information. Consequently, we have no way of knowing what, if any, systematic issues are happening in our application that we might not have thought of and no way of debugging issues that occur in production environments that aren't immediately replicable in lower environments.

This anti-pattern saves time for developers because there is no need for them to apply a structured error-handling approach during development, and it meets the users' need to not see confusing messages. However, it comes with many negative side effects.

Results

The most obvious result of error hiding is that you can't find the error. Errors are systematically hidden, and you have to rely on user reports and your ability to reproduce those in order to address any issues.

Debugging errors in Salesforce without good log information can be extremely hard, especially when the errors may be related to user context, data volumes, or similar variables that aren't easy to control.

That means your maintenance costs will be substantially increased and your cycle time for bug resolution will lengthen. Users are also likely to start losing faith in the system as they find that there may be issues that are swept under the carpet, which can lead to a vicious cycle of users starting to blame all sorts of ailments on hidden system issues.

Eventually, you will need to refactor the application and introduce a systematic approach to logging and error handling. This will generally turn out to be much more expensive than having done things properly the first time.

Better solutions

The solution to error hiding is to adopt a structured approach to error handling, starting at the analysis phase of the project. You should analyze common failure modes and prepare for them proactively rather than simply focusing on the happy path.

You should also have a standard for error handling that includes how to handle exceptions, how to log errors, and how to show error messages to end users in different contexts. You should also adopt a good logging framework. I tend to recommend Nebula (`https://github.com/jongpie/NebulaLogger`) as a framework, but there are many good options available from the community.

When looking for one, keep the following in mind. A good logging framework should be easy to use and configure. It should be able to log from multiple sources (for example, Apex, flows, integrations, and so on), and it should have good performance and not slow down your application. Ideally, you also want to be able to easily visualize errors and follow them across process boundaries.

In all of this, of course, you want to insulate your end users from technical error messages. But you want to do it without resorting to an anti-pattern.

Now, we have covered our final anti-pattern of the chapter and are ready to move on to our key takeaways.

Knowing the takeaways

In this section, we will abstract a bit from the specific patterns and instead try to pull out the wider learning points you can use in your day-to-day work as a Salesforce architect or in preparing for the CTA Review Board.

When architecting Salesforce solutions, you should be mindful of the following:

- Don't rush into a solution based on what your organization usually does. Make careful consideration of options.

- When making a buy-versus-build decision, be careful to count the real TCO of a custom solution including long-term run and maintenance costs.

- Don't design solutions to a specific license set if you can at all avoid it.

- Instead, push for a better commercial deal, different scope, or different license mix.

- You must make assumptions about your user base, but be careful about systematic bias.

- To help mitigate bias, use various consultation methods during development to de-risk.

- Don't become too invested in a new technology. No matter how cool it seems, it's not the answer to everything.

- Automations are a particular pain point in many Salesforce solutions. They should be a particular focus of technical governance.

- Prefer a simpler automation setup to a more complex one.

- If you need a complex custom UX, decompose the functionality in a meaningful way rather than putting everything in a single component.

- When doing substantial development on Salesforce, you should apply all the same good practice that applies to other OO development projects in similar languages. That includes how you structure your classes and how you handle exceptions and errors.

In preparing for the CTA Review Board, you should be mindful of the following:

- Using AppExchange products in your solution is entirely appropriate and usually preferable to custom solutions

- Recommend products you know and can justify or alternately are well-known in the market to avoid unnecessary questions

- Assume that budget is not a constraint and recommend the right licenses for the job

- However, don't go overboard and recommend lots of additional feature licenses if you don't actually need them

- Make assumptions freely, but state them as you go along

- Be prepared for judges to ask you to consider on the fly what would happen if you changed a key assumption

- Recommend the right tool for the job and avoid relying on too one-sided a solutioning approach

- Don't go overboard with automations, and always be clear on what approach you are recommending and why

- Prefer a simpler automation setup to a more complex one

- Recommending custom components is often appropriate, but be careful not to overdo its functionality

- Do remember that when recommending code-based solutions, you should also know good practices for OO development, although it might mainly be relevant during Q&A

- Have a structured error-handling approach in mind that you can tell the judges should they ask

We have now covered the material for this chapter and are ready to proceed. First, however, we will summarize our learning.

Summary

In this chapter, we have covered eight anti-patterns, more than any chapter so far. That is not accidental. Solution architecture is probably the most time-consuming activity for most architects. Even if we aren't directly responsible for all parts of the solution, we get pulled in to consult on features all the time.

Solution architecture is the most visible part of our efforts. While integration architecture, data architecture, and security architecture set the baseline on which we create our solutions, ultimately it is the solution that we devise for the users that is the basis of their judgment.

If we get the core architecture right but fail to deliver a good solution, we will still in the eyes of most observers have failed. Unfortunately, it is also a really hard area to get right.

As these anti-patterns show, keeping the right balance between flexibility and discipline, and between giving the users what they want and adhering to good technical practice, is something that requires experience and good judgment. Hopefully, you now have an even deeper appreciation of that fact.

Having covered solution architecture, we will move on to our next domain: integration architecture.

6

Keeping Integration Straight

This chapter looks at anti-patterns around your integrations with other systems. The first part of the chapter looks at anti-patterns around the integration landscape and integration patterns, the second part looks at what can go wrong in the design and use of interfaces, and the third zooms in on problems with integration styles. As always, we end the chapter by distilling the key takeaways.

In this chapter, we're going to cover the following main topics:

- How not to overly complicate your systems landscape by misusing technologies in ways they weren't intended to
- When it is and isn't appropriate to create custom services for integrations
- How to avoid common failures in designing interfaces
- How to use integration patterns appropriately

After completing this chapter, you will have a good idea about how to better select integration patterns and structure your integration architecture by learning about various ways in which it can go terribly wrong.

Muddling up the integration landscape

This section covers two anti-patterns that in different ways can create havoc in your integration landscape. We will start by looking at how not to use middleware.

Middleware in name only (MINO)

Using middleware to create point-to-point connections rather than using its extended capabilities

Example

PumpCo is a large B2B company that specializes in the production of pumps for industrial production. It operates in more than 30 markets and has historically underinvested in IT systems and used largely manual processes for sales that have varied substantially between countries and product lines.

Over the past year, it has started to implement Salesforce Sales Cloud and CPQ to drive standardization of the sales process globally. Their one major IT platform that has received substantial investment in the past is SAP and, fundamentally, SAP runs all key parts of the business today.

Michelle is brought in as an integration architect on the Salesforce implementation at an early stage. The integration roadmap is very ambitious as the business wants to see all relevant data and processes seamlessly operate across the Salesforce/SAP boundary. Fundamentally, it wants to be able to access all the relevant back-office data and processes directly in Salesforce without the need for a context switch.

When the initial mapping has been completed, there are 75 discrete integration points covering everything from pricing and logistics to HR that would need to be implemented to give the full experience that the business is looking for. The good news, however, is that many of these integration points can be grouped into similar areas such as a **customer or an order interface**.

The architects from the Salesforce and the SAP side discuss a number of alternative architectures and implementation approaches for creating a small number of stable interfaces that would cater to the majority of use cases, but unfortunately, progress is slow and there is no real agreement between stakeholders or architects. There is a large number of potential solutions in play as well as several technologies that could potentially do the job, and the willingness to compromise is low.

The two sides instead agree to let the middleware team manage the process. PumpCo has just bought a new middleware platform, and the team there is looking for opportunities to get started.

The middleware team will expose services to Salesforce and translate the calls to SAP. Any modifications to the APIs will also be its responsibility. Thereby, the two platform teams don't have to agree on an approach and can work independently.

As the project progresses, Michelle makes a count of the interfaces Salesforce is calling on the middleware. She counts 45. Not quite the original 75, but then, the scope has also been somewhat reduced as they have gone along.

Here's a diagram of PumpCo's integration architecture:

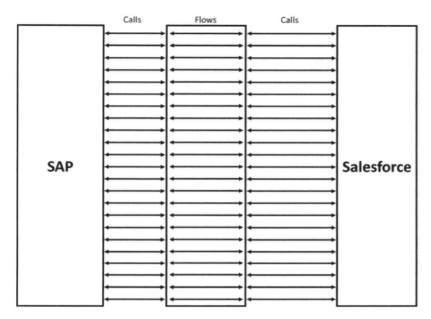

Figure 6.1 – PumpCo integration architecture

From what she can see, most of these middleware interfaces do little other than simply forward a call from Salesforce to SAP and back again. She wonders if that is really the best approach, but it's not her problem anymore.

However, over time as Salesforce starts seeing more use, issues start occurring with the integrations. The error rate is high, there are performance issues, and maintenance is getting increasingly complex. Integrations, overall, are causing the majority of technical issues on the platform.

A consultancy is brought in to assess the situation, and they recommend rationalizing the integration architecture as the current setup effectively consists of 45 increasingly customized point-to-point connections via the middleware. This creates a lot of potential for failure and is generally hard to understand.

Michelle is asked to participate in the redesign process, and after several weeks of design work, they end up with a proposal not too far away from one of the iterations that were done during the initial project implementation. When a senior stakeholder pointedly asks why this wasn't done in the first place, no one is really able to give a convincing answer.

Problem

The MINO anti-pattern tries to reduce the complexity of creating a good integration architecture by introducing middleware. However, it does so in a way that fails to leverage the capabilities of a middleware platform, instead simply recreating flows via the middleware that might have been found in a point-to-point scenario.

It tends to occur in organizations that have complex system landscapes with many interfaces and touchpoints between systems. However, in these organizations, there is often little technical governance coordinating between different silos, leading to a messy integration architecture.

Other characteristics that are often found with the MINO anti-pattern include the presence of dated and inflexible system APIs on key platforms and difficulty in agreeing on standard representations of core business entities across those key platforms, making it impossible to settle on common interfaces or APIs.

Proposed solution

The solution proposed by MINO is simply to introduce a middleware platform without paying too close attention to how it is used. By introducing a modern middleware platform, the complexities and inflexibilities of legacy systems can at least be partially hidden, which does lead to good initial results.

That is to say, MINO often seems right on the surface, but if the middleware implementation only replicates the existing mess in a new format, relatively little is gained. Not nothing, mind you. You may still get some basic middleware capabilities such as better error logging, a retry mechanism, or some easier-to-use protocol conversion.

Another and often more influential reason to go down the road of this anti-pattern is that it decouples teams on core platforms from having to deal directly with each other. You can often have very different views of the world if you're working on the CRM side than if you are working on the ERP side of a key integration.

MINO allows different teams to only have to deal with the common middleware team, who are then given the responsibility for managing the rest. That, unfortunately, tends to lead to architectures that don't really move much beyond the basics.

Results

The result of MINO is often turning your system landscape into an even greater spaghetti-like mess than it was before. Now, after all, you have a middleware in the center, so you can pay less attention.

That has the usual consequences:

- Hard-to-understand integration architecture with too many individual interfaces and point-to-point connections, albeit mediated by the middleware

- Increased maintenance costs as the complexity is still high and there are now more teams involved

- Lack of technical governance and a potential lack of awareness that such governance is even needed

- Increasing error rates on integrations and a commensurately increased fix time as teams try to track down errors across platforms

- Decreasing performance as there is a more complex flow in place that spans more platforms

Overall, if all you are going to do with your middleware is proxy point-to-point connections, you are probably better off not using it at all.

Better solutions

What the MINO anti-pattern teaches is that there is no shortcut you can take to get your integration architecture right. You have to carefully consider the linkages and dependencies between systems, the business requirements both today and going forward, how your master data is distributed, which core capabilities your key platforms have, and how you can structure interfaces and patterns to best support all these elements.

Some common middleware capabilities are shown in the following diagram:

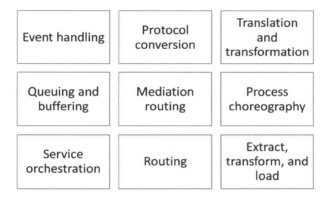

Figure 6.2 – Common middleware capabilities

With that in mind, you can select the right tools for the job, which may very well be a middleware tool. However, before you have thought about which interfaces you will need to support across the business, which integration patterns you can and must support for different scenarios, and determined how you are going to do technical governance across different teams, you shouldn't be jumping at any tool, no matter how cool it looks.

Service proliferation syndrome

Creating a solution based on a license set that you can afford rather than the license set you really need without making the necessary compromises

Example

OmniCo has always prided itself on being at the forefront of technology and deploys many cutting-edge software platforms across its many diversified service lines. The company was an early adopter of **service-oriented architecture (SOA)**, which it still uses to great advantage combined with an **event-driven architecture** (EDA) for high-velocity data and processes.

OmniCo is now implementing Salesforce as a replacement for its old Siebel CRM system, which served as an integration hub for many other systems. The Siebel CRM was heavily customized to OmniCo processes, and the company is expecting that the new Salesforce system will be as well. While their implementation partner has made a reasoned argument for staying with standard capabilities, this goes against the grain of how OmniCo has historically done things, and it is not really looking to change its approach as part of the CRM project.

Here's what the old Siebel setup looked like:

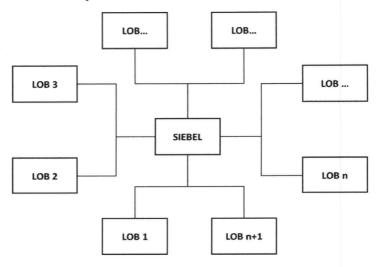

Figure 6.3 – Old Siebel setup at OmniCo

For Erhat, the consulting manager in charge of the integration part of the implementation project, this is causing a lot of anxiety. He is being pushed by a number of senior stakeholders from OmniCo toward building a range of special business services that would fit into the OmniCo SOA.

Erhat has tried building customized APIs on vanilla Salesforce in the past, and the experience, while ultimately successful, was neither straightforward nor fast. In fact, given the number of custom services that are being mentioned, he is in doubt about the basic feasibility, given constraints on time, budget, and people with the necessary skillsets.

After some pushback, he agrees with stakeholders to deliver two crucial services using interfaces similar to the ones exposed by the old Siebel system that are used in order management and that would take a lot of time to re-engineer on a different pattern.

These are delivered, but prove difficult to get through testing, partially because the testing protocols for the services are incomplete and partially because the complexity is extraordinarily high.

As the first two services near completion, a crisis meeting is called by OmniCo's enterprise architecture board. They have just realized that not all the business services provided by Siebel will be available in the new Salesforce setup. In the view of several members of the board, this will fundamentally undermine a range of business processes as other systems would need to change their integration approach substantially or switch to manual processing of certain steps.

Erhat, not knowing the processes at OmniCo very well, finds himself unable to argue on the merits of the case. The members of the board present him with definitions for an additional 13 services that cover different parts of the Lead-to-Cash process and that were available in the previous Siebel setup. Here's a schematic view of the integrations:

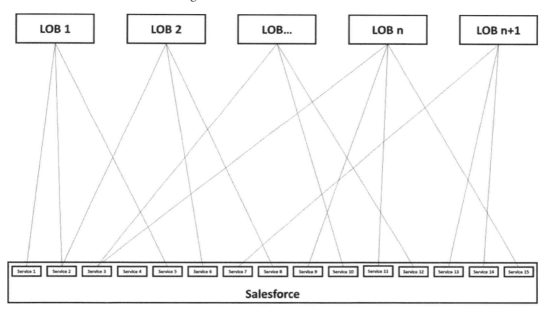

Figure 6.4 – Schematic view of OmniCo Salesforce integrations, not including ESB

Erhat can only really push back on a practical level, which he does arguing that the services are outside scope, are not included in pricing, and that he doesn't have the team to deliver. OmniCo grumbles a bit and there are a few escalation meetings. However, Erhat is eventually told not to worry—they will solve it some other way.

That way turns out to be bringing in a team of disparate contractors to quickly build the services alongside the main consulting partner's team. Erhat can just wait and observe as the contractors run into the inevitable technical complexities. He leaves the project prior to go-live with something of a bad taste in his mouth.

12 months later, he is back at OmniCo. He has been brought in as an expert on the company's Salesforce APIs, which have proved very error-prone and expensive to maintain.

OmniCo is looking for the rationale for why it was built like this in the first place and what to do to fix it. It is also considering different approaches such as changing integration patterns or bringing in some middleware. Erhat takes a deep breath and starts planning the analysis.

Problem

The problem that service proliferation syndrome revolves around is how to fit Salesforce into an existing enterprise architecture that will have preexisting expectations of the capabilities delivered by its key systems. That may be an SOA, as in our example, or a different organizing principle, but typically, one that requires very specific things from key platforms.

This anti-pattern is common across a variety of platforms as it will potentially affect any newcomer to an integration landscape. In the past, it would have been more common as organizations were busily building SOAs, often without a lot of thought as to the organization of specific services.

Today, it is perhaps most commonly encountered when old systems are replaced and interfaces are required that don't quite fit with the standard capabilities of built-in system APIs. While Salesforce has extensive APIs, they are very data model-centric, and many integration architectures are built along different principles such as coarse-grained business services, which aren't aligned at all.

Proposed solution

Service proliferation syndrome tackles the problem of fitting into the integration landscape by writing as many and as complex services directly on the Salesforce platform to accommodate the various requests that may be encountered.

This is another anti-pattern that can seem deceptively rational as you are, after all, directly delivering business value and sometimes in line with expectations from cross-company technical governance forums. Therefore, you can be under a lot of pressure to go down this route, knowing full well the damage it is going to do to your platform in the long run.

Because the capabilities are there on the platform and the need is there in the enterprise environment, fighting this anti-pattern can sometimes be impossible. This is even more true because the costs only really accumulate over time.

Results

The first issue you are likely to see with service proliferation syndrome is increased complexity and increased build costs. Custom services on Salesforce, while feasible and sometimes the right choice, are complex to get right. Salesforce isn't inherently an API platform, a good reason for the acquisition of MuleSoft a few years back.

The increased complexity will over time lead to increased maintenance costs and not just on Salesforce. The various teams using the proliferation of services may also face ongoing costs to rework and upgrade their connections.

Sometimes, a custom service can be the right choice, and the benefits can outstrip the costs both for the initial build and for the maintenance. That is rarely—if ever—the case for 15 custom services as in our example. If you think you need that, you probably need to rethink your approach.

Better solutions

The first piece of advice is to start by looking at standard integration patterns to see if you can find a standard piece of technology that fits the bill. Maybe there is a way of using standard APIs. Maybe you can use a batch process. Maybe you can emit events and have other systems subscribe to those.

You should look broadly and not immediately jump to a custom interface, even if that seems like a good initial fit. The danger is that you go for the gold-plated solution, not realizing the real long-run costs of the decision.

If you do decide that a large number of custom APIs are required—and there are situations where that can be justified—you should use a platform that is built for this purpose to implement. MuleSoft would be the canonical choice for Salesforce, but there are others in the marketplace that can fill this niche.

Overall, you run a risk of overcomplicating both your Salesforce interface and your integration landscape by indiscriminately building services. As always, consider the hard trade-offs and make a decision based on a real view of pros and cons.

Interfacing indecently

In this section, we will look at two common anti-patterns that affect the design of integrations at a concrete level. The first, fat interface, looks at a problem with interface design, while the second, chatty integration, looks at a problem with how interfaces are used.

Fat interface

When a single interface starts doing too many things, you run into a host of problems.

Example

Joe works as an integration architect for a small Salesforce partner that specializes in complex implementations often requiring substantial amounts of code or other kinds of customization. He has just started a new contract with RealCo, a major real estate investment company that uses Salesforce as the key system of engagement across the entire business.

The work he is initially contracted to do includes building a custom interface for accessing information about valuations, which is used by RealCo's partners as part of making deals. The information is held in RealCo's Salesforce org and needs to be available in real time.

Joe sets up the API constituting the interface on RealCo's middleware platform and orchestrates calls to a few different Salesforce standard APIs and a single custom one as part of the implementation. However, close to the go-live of the new interface, a bunch of new use cases drops on his desk.

These include not just extensions to the valuation API, such as getting historical valuations and trend data, but also entirely different categories of property data including information about the structure of the building, access to key metrics from various assessments, and information on feedback from viewings conducted by RealCo partners.

Joe pushes back a bit on the customer, saying that if he'd known that this much new functionality would be coming, he might have structured the API differently and might have done some things in a suboptimal way to include it with the current go-live.

RealCo's manager listens attentively to Joe but says that ultimately, the decision is to go ahead with the additional functionality. RealCo is aware of the potential downsides, and it can live with them.

The day before the go-live, the same thing happens again. This time, the information includes more property-related information but also entirely different classes of information such as demographics and segmentation data related to the area in which the property is located, as illustrated in the following diagram:

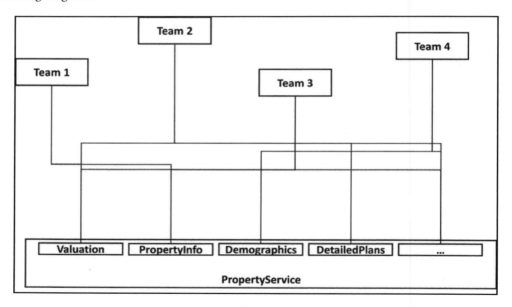

Figure 6.5 – View of RealCo PropertyService

Nothing can be done to include this in a day, which RealCo begrudgingly accepts. However, it wants a plan from Joe to include it post-haste. Given the immense pressure, Joe simply extends the current interface, which is now becoming enormous with calls to dozens of Salesforce services, both standard and custom.

Fortunately, both the initial go-live and the subsequent update go relatively well. The teams at RealCo's partner organizations grumble a bit about the complexity of the interface and log a number of bugs. But it works, and they can get on with the various applications that the interface needs to drive.

The barrage of change requests keeps happening. And somehow, the changes are always exceptionally urgent and needed for critical use cases in one partner or another. What's worse is that an increasing number of teams are relying on the interface, which makes upgrades increasingly hard.

Even with good API versioning, the changes between versions are proving quite strenuous for the partner teams who are complaining quite loudly both about the frequent version changes and about the high error rate that has crept into the API implementation.

The final straw comes when a critical bug is found just prior to a new release. Joe, having been told to prioritize getting the new functionality out, includes a hotfix with the new version, which effectively forces an upgrade on all the major partners.

However, it turns out that there are additional breaking bugs in the new API version, which means the key partners lose access to key functionality for over a week until Joe can get the situation under control.

An escalation meeting is called where the partners can voice their various complaints. Joe tries as best he can to explain the history and the reasons for the current situation, but unfortunately, the complexities get lost in the general din.

Joe is told that his contract won't be renewed and that another consultancy will be brought in to refactor and restructure the interface. He draws a sigh of relief and starts looking forward to his next engagement.

Problem

The problem addressed by the fat interface is fundamentally one of the interface structure—that is to say, where to place functionality so that it can be called by clients that have a need for the services the interface provides.

> **Note**
>
> Originally, this anti-pattern was applied more to interfaces in the sense of the word used in **object-oriented programming (OOP)**. However, it applies equally in an integration setting.

There are several different philosophies on interface design. These days, most people have an instinctual preference for microservices, smallish services that carry out a single well-defined and coherent set of functionalities. An example could be a notification service that does nothing but send notifications.

A few years back, however, the preference was for coarse-grained business services that provided an entry point to a business process—for example, processing an order. This was the foundational style associated with SOA, which we mentioned previously.

With fat interface, however, you are violating a fundamental tenet of interface design that is common to most—if not—all these philosophies. That tenet is called interface segregation and holds that clients should never be forced to depend on methods that it doesn't need.

Proposed solution

Fat interface proposes to simply continue to add logic to an existing interface because it is the easiest thing to do. Designing well-segregated interfaces can take work and careful thought, and putting all your functionality into a single basket simplifies the problem.

In addition, you can sometimes convince yourself that all the functionality really does belong together because there are some tangential commonalities between it, and this can be especially true if you have consumers that use substantial parts of the functionality you expose.

Often, this anti-pattern is simply the consequence of drift over time. The code starts to do one thing, then it does another, and another, and at the end of the day it does everything and walks the dog.

That would be well and good if it weren't for the fact that it comes with a number of hidden costs that have to be taken into account. These we'll explore next.

Results

The results of the fat interface anti-pattern will be familiar if you have been reading this book straight through. It resembles the consequences of poor structure that can occur in a multitude of domains.

When your interface has grown to the extent that it becomes a fat interface—that is to say it now includes so much diverse functionality to have become effectively unmanageable—you are likely to see some or all of the following consequences:

- Increased complexity, leading to increased cost of change, increased cycle times, and increased error rates
- Increased maintenance costs as errors have additional repercussions, clients depend on a variety of existing parts of the interface, and the code base is large and hard to understand
- Only certain developers can make changes to the fat interface because the interdependencies and consequences to users of the interface of making changes require in-depth knowledge of the entire code base
- Bugs in the interface can affect clients that do not even use the kind of functionality exposed in the failing method
- A large number of client dependencies on the interface make disentangling the status quo difficult

Overall, this pattern can seem like a minor code smell when you are just having a quick look. In fact, it can create serious issues for your company-wide integration landscape if you have a failing fat interface in a central position.

Better solutions

This anti-pattern is one of the few that can consistently be avoided by applying good practice and discipline to your development processes. If you diligently follow your interface standards and apply the interface segregation principle whenever you are adding new functionality, this anti-pattern will never occur.

While it may be tempting to take shortcuts and they might not have serious consequences in the short term, you should know the long-term consequences and apply sound design and programming practice. This is also an area where an architect or developer may have a lot to say as it is too technical an area for most business users to really take a position.

The difficulty is, of course, to maintain the required level of discipline when you are under serious pressure to deliver. However, hopefully, making the kinds of points raised in this description will help you push back on quick-fix thinking.

Chatty integration

Chatty integration is an anti-pattern where integration of arbitrary patterns makes an unduly large number of calls to one or more interfaces, often resulting in performance degradation.

Example

WoodCo is a furniture maker with a long legacy of making top-tier bespoke furniture for well-off clients. It has been growing like wildfire for the past years due to the launch of an e-commerce platform, built on Salesforce Experience Cloud with B2B commerce, that connects their customer community directly with furniture makers assigned to their projects.

That way, customers and makers can connect directly and discuss requirements for the bespoke builds. Customers can also follow the progress of their furniture throughout its life cycle.

WoodCo project manages the builds, including the budgets, and ensures that any conflicts are resolved amicably wherever possible. It tracks these projects in an old project control module that it also uses to manage its own business.

This project module has recently been extended with a custom-built REST API that sits on top of the legacy application. The vendor has built this API specifically for WoodCo at great expense, but it's considered a no-brainer as it will allow the direct integration of the portal into the project control module, replacing the current manual process where everything is rekeyed into the project control module by data entry professionals.

Lina is hired by WoodCo to head up digital projects, the first of which is to connect the e-commerce platform to the project control module. She commissions a specialist Salesforce partner to lead the work.

They put in place a lightweight middleware platform that subscribes to events from Salesforce and translates them into REST calls in the format of the new REST API. The REST API doesn't support any aggregation, so it's strictly one event to one call.

On the Salesforce side, events are initially only fired on status updates or when key pieces of standing information such as a project title are entered or changed. However, over time, this should be extended to tracking the status of activities within the project and the communication between maker and customer.

You can see an overview of the WoodCo integration architecture here:

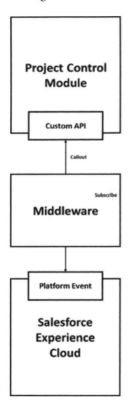

Figure 6.6 – WoodCo integration architecture

The integration launches successfully, and everyone in WoodCo cheers. However, the full benefit is not yet realized as the activities and customer communication are still only in the customer portal, and WoodCo staff still use a combination of rekeying and working in multiple systems to get around the constraint.

Finally, the day of the update, which will include the full synchronization, arrives and everybody waits excitedly for the go-live. However, within minutes of the launch, the project module crashes.

The vendor investigates and attributes the error to scalability issues related to the initial synchronization. The rollout is deferred to the weekend, and after many restarts, the initial data is indeed synchronized.

Monday comes, and people start using the system in anger. There are some complaints about slowness in the project control module, but at least the integration seems to be working and bringing the critical data across.

Then, on Tuesday morning, an administrator is running some routine batch jobs on the customer portal. Near instantly, the project control module comes crashing down again and the new integration is taken offline in order to get it back up.

A crisis meeting is called for that evening by WoodCo's CIO. This has reached the level of CEO attention, and something needs to be done. Lina entrusts Aki, her most technically gifted subordinate, to figure out the root cause.

At this point, both vendors are blaming each other for the failure and are digging their heels in, refusing to take unilateral action to fix the problem. Aki, therefore, dives right into the middle of the technical setup.

He examines log files and code from Salesforce, the middleware, and the project control module, and after a few hours, he is confident that he has found the root cause. The problem is caused by a recursive update rule that applies certain updates to a parent project such as a change of billing code to all activities in that project's scope.

Before the new update, this didn't matter as changes on the activity level weren't synchronized. However, with the update, each such change triggers hundreds of update events on Salesforce, each of which triggers a callout to the project control module.

You can see an overview of the WoodCo project structure here:

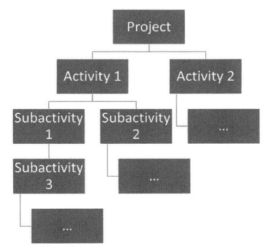

Figure 6.7 – WoodCo project structure

This legacy system can handle maybe one or two such updates at the same time while also serving users normally, but anything more than that causes issues—first, performance degradation, and eventually, a crash. When the administrator launched a batch job to reassign a number of **project identifiers (PIDs)**, this triggered updates for dozens of projects and their activity trees, crashing the project control module in the process.

At the evening's meeting, the mood is somber. However, as Aki explains the facts of the matter, no one can really disagree. The decision is taken to temporarily disable the activity level and for Aki to lead a team to redesign the integration so that it avoids overloading the project control module.

Problem

The chatty integration anti-pattern is a byproduct of the solution to some other integration problem that for some reason requires very frequent communication between systems. Often, as in our example, that problem involves the transfer of state between two or more systems.

It is an anti-pattern that can be hard to spot during development as it tends to only become problematic with scale. After all, in most test scenarios, except explicit performance tests, we don't update enough data to really reach a problematic number of integration calls.

The problematic implementation can be due to bad practices such as firing separate callouts for every record in a loop, or it can be more insidious, as in our example, where subscribed events are mapped 1:1 to REST calls in the middleware. Whichever way it occurs, it is at best wasteful and at worst catastrophic.

Proposed solution

As noted, chatty integration tends to be a byproduct of the solution to another problem, therefore it doesn't quite fit our schema. However, in so far as we can say it proposes a solution, that solution is to make as many calls across system boundaries as necessary to support the business use case without any concern for system limitations.

This is usually done for reasons of simplicity. Once you start introducing bulkification, queuing, systematic delays, aggregation of calls, throttling, or any other mechanism you might consider to limit the rate of calling other interfaces, you also introduce complexity in the implementation.

You will have noted from other anti-patterns that complexity is often a driver of serious negative consequences, so avoiding it will usually seem like a good thing. This, however, is a case where the adage *make the solution as simple as possible but no simpler* applies.

With chatty integration, you are actually making the solution too simple as it doesn't meet the basic functional requirement without the additional complexity. That may mean you need more time and additional tools to get your solution to work, but there really is no way around it in this kind of scenario.

This is still true even when using low-code integration tools, sold to make your life easy. If you get the integration strategy wrong, the integration won't work as intended. Architecture is about trade-offs, after all.

Results

The results of chatty integration form a spectrum:

- Often, there are no immediate consequences if the target systems are able to cope with the extraordinary volume of calls and you stay within Salesforce limits as well.

- Sometimes, you see performance degradation. That can happen on the Salesforce side if you make too many async callouts over a time period, and it can obviously happen on the target side if you start overloading its capacity.

- Performance degradation can turn into periodic errors if you start experiencing timeouts or the target servers get temporarily overloaded.

- Finally, you can sometimes crash the target system altogether, leading to a critical error

You can refer to the following diagram for a visual demonstration:

Chatty integration, spectrum of consequences

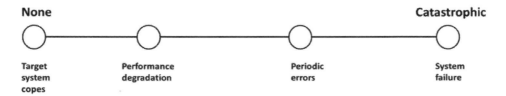

Figure 6.8 – Chatty integration spectrum

That doesn't mean this isn't an anti-pattern if you happen to be lucky enough to be on the left side of the spectrum. It just means that for now, you got away with it.

Better solutions

The general advice to follow in order to avoid the chatty integration anti-pattern is to understand and design with system limits in mind. We are not creating theoretical architectures for theoretical systems. If we were, we would be in academia.

When you design an integration as an architect, you are generally doing so with a well-defined target environment in mind. That means you should be mindful of the following:

- Understand the hard constraints such as system limits—for example, the maximum number of calls supported over a time period

- Get information on the actual performance of target systems under whatever level of duress they currently experience

- Don't just fire off calls without consideration of the performance implications of doing so

Instead, use one or more of the following strategies to ensure that the target system can cope:

- **Bulkification**: Send multiple logical calls in the same message

- **Consolidation**: Combine multiple updates in a single call

- **Aggregation**: Combine changes to multiple areas into one call covering several areas

- **Delay**: Introduce a delay in sending off a call when performance is spiky

- **Reduce frequency**: Send updates less often

- **Buffer**: Add your calls to a queue that is gradually drained as the target system has capacity

Overall, a chatty integration has the potential to level your integration landscape if you are unlucky. Therefore, it should be avoided even when you don't believe you will run into trouble in the short term.

Getting the patterns wrong

In this section, we look at how becoming too obsessed with a single integration style can cause serious problems by looking at the integration pattern monomania anti-pattern.

Integration pattern monomania

> *Integration pattern monomania happens when a single integration pattern is used to the exclusion of all others, regardless of whether it is a good fit for the requirements under consideration.*

Example

WineCo has been a heavy user of Salesforce technology for more than a decade. It has a large estate of many orgs across core clouds, Marketing Cloud, and commerce.

It has developed a custom approach to building on Salesforce, including a range of frameworks and libraries that it uses consistently across projects. Many of these could use an update, but they are still preferred for the sake of consistency.

Clare is brought in from a leading consultancy to lead the build of a new app that WineCo is building for its distributors. The app will include communications between WineCo managers and the distributors, e-commerce for standard items, rebate management, custom pricing logic, joint opportunity management, and the ability to request quotes for special requirements.

To deliver the required level of functionality and realize the business value attributed to the distributor portal, Clare will need to ensure that integrations are in place to many systems.

She must funnel all communications through the central notification service that ensures all communications are appropriately logged and have the right footers in place. Then, she must integrate with the existing rebate management system that calculates the rebates due to distributors based on their segment and historical orders.

Pricing will come from Salesforce CPQ but in a different org, requiring a Salesforce-to-Salesforce integration. Content for the portal web pages will come from the corporate CMS. However, there are also services for user and behavior tracking that must be integrated from the CMS into the portal website.

Finally, the ERP needs to be updated with any custom quotes and standard orders that are made through the distributor portal. The distributor portal will also need to get a substantial amount of data about distributors, their existing orders, and standing data about them from the ERP. All in all, while the basic build on Salesforce is complex, the integration landscape is even more complex.

The proposed architecture is represented in the following diagram:

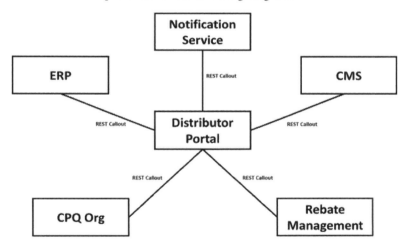

Figure 6.9 – Proposed integration architecture for WineCo

Further complexity is added by WineCo's corporate integration standard. It states that all integrations from Salesforce must be implemented using the company's integration library. That would be fine; however, the only patterns supported by this library are synchronous or asynchronous REST callouts, limiting the options for the integration design considerably.

Clare and her team get on with it, regardless. They complete much of the core Salesforce build ahead of schedule, but the integrations are lagging behind. They run into several different problems.

First, the rebate system doesn't support any kind of bulkification, leading to large numbers of calls to its APIs. The system owner questions whether the current setup will scale in a go-live scenario, and eventually, four new servers need to be procured to give the business comfort that the system can handle the load.

Second, there are too many queries to the ERP system, leading to slow response time and long wait times in the UI. This proves unsolvable under the current architecture, and a decision is made to handle it as a training issue.

Third, the CMS services prove hard to call from the server side, and a compromise is made to include the tracking code via JavaScript, although this requires a formal exception and causes substantial delay.

Finally, the notification service is a bad fit for many of the messaging requirements that the distributor portal has and results in weirdly formatted messages that are hard to reply to in many cases. That is also accepted and consigned to be handled as a training issue.

The project is completed and goes live without much fanfare. The internal users dislike the new interface and distributor adoption is lukewarm. Clare makes a final argument for redesigning the basic integration architecture to something more suitable, before moving on to the next project.

Problem

Integration pattern monomania seeks to address the problem that designing a good integration architecture is fundamentally hard, as is determining the right patterns, design, and implementation characteristics of concrete integrations.

It is, therefore, attempting to simplify the problem by focusing on a single approach that works well in many cases. That way, you can define a standard way of doing things without having to grapple with the exact details of each individual case.

This is attractive for several reasons:

- First, standards often work. In many cases, having a standard way of doing things is the right way to go. However, an entire integration architecture is too broad a target for such an approach.

- Second, once you have chosen an approach, you can create supporting assets such as code libraries, frameworks for logging and error handling, and so on that will work across integrations, which is generally beneficial.

- Third, you only really need developers to know how to do a single thing. That reduces development complexity, training, and onboarding needs.

All of that would be great if it weren't for the inconvenient fact that no single integration pattern is universally applicable.

Proposed solution

Integration pattern monomania proposes to use a single integration pattern for all—or at least, nearly all—concrete integrations needed in an integration architecture. It can be either explicitly set via a corporate standard or it can be implicit in the way the architects and developers work and think. In either case, when such a preference becomes excessively strong, you have an anti-pattern.

The aims of integration pattern monomania are usually eminently sensible:

- Reducing the complexity of integrations by limiting the choices architects and developers need to make

- Enforcing consistency in the enterprise architecture to avoid unwanted side effects

- Make developers' lives easier by giving them a clear way forward and supporting them with relevant tools and frameworks

The issue is that not all concrete integrations will fit a given pattern. Characteristics such as the velocity of updates, acceptable latency, data volumes, and the needs of the **user experience** (**UX**), among other concerns, mean that overreliance on a single integration pattern is detrimental in the long term. This we will explore next.

Results

The problems caused by integration pattern monomania boil down to technical misfits. This is something we have seen in other anti-patterns—for instance, Golden Hammer. While some of the positives may apply in specific cases, overall you are likely to see some of the following consequences:

- Instead of decreasing complexity as intended, your integration landscape becomes more complex due to a variety of workarounds needed to accommodate the limitations of the integration pattern that is being used exclusively.

- Some integrations may not function within their intended quality parameters because of poor technical fit. That may mean periodic errors, poor performance, or similar.

- These factors generally imply a higher maintenance and support burden on an ongoing basis to correct the issues.

- Finally, the UX in some areas will be underwhelming to end users as the pattern can't meet expectations.

Overall, you don't get the anticipated benefits and instead end up with a bit of a mess.

Better solutions

The solution to integration pattern monomania is simple. Don't get overly fixated on a single integration pattern, whether that is RESTful callouts, EDA, or batch transfers.

Instead, you can give good guidance to application developers and architects about which patterns are appropriate in which circumstances. It is fine to have a preference where all else is equal, but in practice, things rarely are.

Here's an overview of Salesforce integration patterns:

Integration from Salesforce

Type	Timing	Preferred Pattern
Process Integration	Synchronous	Remote Process Invocation—Request and Reply
Process Integration	Asynchronous	Remote Process Invocation—Fire and Forget
Data Integration	Synchronous	Remote Process Invocation—Request and Reply
Data Integration	Asynchronous	UI Update Based on Data Changes
Virtual Integration	Synchronous	Data Virtualization

Integration to Salesforce

Type	Timing	Preferred
Process Integration	Synchronous	Remote Call-In
Process Integration	Asynchronous	Remote Call-In
Data Integration	Synchronous	Remote Call-In
Data Integration	Asynchronous	Batch Data Synchronization

Figure 6.10 – Overview of Salesforce integration patterns

A certain level of conservatism toward choosing integration patterns can be warranted. That can give you some of the benefits that come from having a consistent approach, such as leveraging standard frameworks and libraries.

You can also use middleware to create a certain commonality of integration stance between systems, although that just moves the complexity onto another platform. However, when push comes to shove, if a certain approach is the right one for your integration, then you should use it.

We have now completed our coverage of the patterns in this chapter and will continue to the key takeaways.

Knowing the takeaways

In this section, we will abstract a bit from the specific patterns and instead try to pull out the wider learning points you can use in your day-to-day work as a Salesforce architect or in preparing for the CTA Review Board.

When architecting Salesforce solutions, you should be mindful of the following:

- Middleware can be a great way to create order and improve the structure of your system landscape. However, you can also use it in ways that do more harm than good.

- If all you are doing is replacing point-to-point connections with equivalent one-to-one flows through the middleware, you are probably in anti-pattern territory.

- Custom services can be a great addition to your Salesforce org in certain cases. However, they come with considerable added complexity.

- You should never reflexively add lots of custom services because they seem to be what the business is calling for. Instead, take a step back and look at the big picture of requirements to see what options you have for realizing the specific integration flows required.

- If you are building custom interfaces, whether on Salesforce or on your middleware platform, have appropriate governance in place to avoid ending up with a fat interface that does everything.

- Avoid excessively frequent integration calls if possible.

- If you do need high-frequency state transfer, consider using a dedicated technology such as **Change Data Capture** (**CDC**).

- In general, always design integrations with system limitations explicitly considered. Don't assume an old ERP can handle unlimited calls, for example. Salesforce, of course, also has defined limits.

- Keep a flexible approach to integration architecture. Don't fall in love with a particular style and use it for everything. Just because event-driven microservices are hot doesn't mean they are right for every scenario.

- Do give good guidance on how to select integration patterns for both members of your team and external partners. Don't assume that they will make the right decisions by themselves.

In preparing for the CTA Review Board, you should be mindful of the following:

- Almost every scenario will have a requirement for middleware. You should know the key capabilities of common platforms such as MuleSoft and be able to talk intelligently about how they fit into the system landscape.

- While you may not see enough integrations to create a problem along the lines of the MINO pattern in the scenario, it is still worth thinking about the specific value the middleware is adding to each of the integration flows you are funneling through it.

- Don't reflexively just funnel every integration through the middleware—there are often exceptions that may require different treatment.

- Suggesting a custom web service is a major piece of customization and would need a strong justification to include in a review board architecture.

- If you need a custom interface, it is more likely that you should be building and exposing via the middleware in most scenarios.

- While you are not likely to face a situation with a fat interface in a review board situation, it is worth considering how you are structuring your integration interfaces and whether it is balanced.

- You need to consider the potential performance implications of the designs you suggest. Often, scenarios will have high-volume requirements that if specified in an obvious way will lead to performance issues similar to the chatty integration pattern.

- You may get quizzed on integration limits for the Salesforce platform, so it's worth having these memorized for the board.

- You should know all the common integration patterns on the Salesforce platform inside out.

- This includes the decision guidance on when to choose what pattern. You are likely to need several at the board, and you should be able to clearly articulate why you have chosen as you have.

We have now covered the material for this chapter and are ready to proceed. First, however, we will summarize our learning.

Summary

In this chapter, we have reviewed five different anti-patterns that in very diverse ways can contribute to failing integration architecture. This diversity is worth keeping in mind.

The integration domain is exceedingly complex and there is scope for getting things wrong at multiple levels. From choosing the wrong integration patterns or misusing your middleware to the technical details of your concrete implementation, there are anti-patterns that can potentially cause serious problems not just to your own project but at an enterprise architecture level.

This fertile soil for error is why experienced architects are always wary about integrations. They are one of the most common causes of project failures, both on Salesforce and in general.

It's worth reiterating that this chapter is the only one where all the anti-patterns apply not just to Salesforce but to all enterprise software systems. Having covered this material, you are hopefully slightly better prepared to tackle the challenges ahead of you in the integration domain.

Having now covered the integration domain, we will continue to talk about anti-patterns that apply to your deployment processes and governance.

Part 3: Process and Communication Anti-Patterns

Part 3 will teach you how to identify and mitigate anti-patterns around process, governance, and communication.

This part has the following chapters:

7

Keeping the Development Life Cycle from Going off Track

In this chapter, we will look at anti-patterns related to areas such as development process, governance, and DevOps. We will start by tackling a few significant process-level anti-patterns and then move on to one that deals with DevOps and packaging. Finally, we will tackle a common and very unfortunate anti-pattern related to testing. At the end of the chapter, we will summarize the key takeaways for real life and the CTA Review Board.

In this chapter, we're going to cover the following main topics:

- How you can avoid big-picture mistakes in the delivery of your project such as how you structure releases and deal with key trade-offs

- How to avoid structuring your packages in a way that may be organizationally convenient but architecturally problematic

- How you can avoid falling into the trap of compromising on code and deployment quality when under pressure to deliver

After completing this chapter, you will have understood the ways in which common mistakes affect the development life cycle and related activities and mastered some tools to help you keep that from happening.

Misaligning the process

In this section, we will look at two anti-patterns that in different ways make the development life cycle go off the rails. First, we will look at how big bang releases can lead to disastrous outcomes in many cases. Second, we will look at project pieism—the disastrous belief that you can avoid making important trade-offs.

Big bang release

The big bang release anti-pattern places the release of all functionalities in a single event at the end of a long-running project.

Example

RollerCo, a major manufacturer of roller skates and skateboards, is going through a major business transformation centered on creating a digitally enabled business that better meets the needs of today's buyers. While not the end-all and be-all of the transformation, several system replacement projects are planned as part of the journey to provide more agility on the IT side.

Anandh is leading the project that aims to replace the legacy, home-grown CRM that RollerCo has been using for the past 15 years. The system will be replaced with a combination of Salesforce Sales and Service Cloud, but due to the high level of customization in the legacy system, it has proven impossible to keep the Salesforce design close to standard.

Another consequence of the high-level customization required is that the entire system will need to go live as a single unit. It won't be possible to release smaller **minimum viable product** (**MVP**) increments prior to full go-live as that would make life too complex for the customer support staff.

Shortly after the project kick-off, Anandh is informed that the board of directors has OKed an **Enterprise Resource Planning** (**ERP**) upgrade to SAP S4/HANA. As the CRM and ERP are closely coupled for several processes, that means that not only will Anandh have to contend with an increased integration backlog, but the rollout plans for the two systems will also need to be coordinated so that both can go live at the same time.

It quickly turns out that the added complexity from the ERP upgrade means the original Salesforce implementation plans will have to slip. In particular, the integrations are proving to be more complex than anyone anticipated.

The CIO, after meeting a trusted vendor representative, announces that to address the issues regarding the CRM/ERP integration, RollerCo will invest in a new strategic middleware platform. This will replace the legacy middleware and go-live with the overall CRM/ERP timeline.

While Anandh and his team are busy redesigning all the integrations to fit with the new middleware platform, yet another discovery is made. The team responsible for RollerCo's web shop determines that it will be next to impossible to get it to work with the new CRM/ERP setup.

It would require changing the fundamental architecture of the application's data layer, and the developer who built that years ago is no longer with the company. No one else is able to figure out how to do it, so a new e-commerce application is also added to the overall program backlog. For convenience, the timeline is aligned with the overall CRM/ERP rollout:

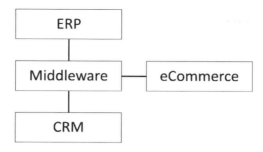

Figure 7.1 – RollerCo new platform

The program suffers never-ending delays. While some areas suffer more than others, none of the major platforms comes out of the implementation phase looking good. Three years go by, and finally, an initial release is nearing completion.

RollerCo has built an elaborate deployment pipeline and cutover plan to be able to handle the multi-system go-live, all slated to happen during a weekend in the company's low season. The testing prior to go-live takes more than 3 months to complete and requires a number of scope reductions and hotfixes.

Even after that, no one in the project dares say unequivocally that the system will work as expected. The number of moving parts is simply too large.

The go-live weekend starts promisingly, with successful completion of required data migration activities. However, as soon as real business users are brought into the systems, issues start cropping up.

By Sunday night, the number of issues has reached a volume that makes going forward seem excessively risky. While no individual issue has so far been a showstopper, the total disruption caused by small issues is significant. On a late-night call, the steering committee takes the decision to roll back and postpone go-live.

The fallout is significant. After all, the program has already had 3 years to complete its work. However, it quickly becomes clear that the issues cannot be fixed in a matter of weeks. There is still much to be done.

The teams come together to find a solution over the next 6 months. Through this period, they focus on reducing the scope and simplifying features to make the rollout process easier to manage.

Eventually, the combined platform with CRM, ERP, middleware, and e-commerce goes live. However, it does so with a large list of known issues and workarounds and a much-reduced scope from the one originally designed.

Problem

Big bang release is an anti-pattern that usually tries to solve the problem of how to handle complex dependencies in the release process. That can be dependencies between systems or inside them. It most frequently occurs where the digital transformation lacks strong leadership, and the leadership that there is highly risk-averse.

Dependencies are usually linked to certain business processes that have a legacy of being carried out in a certain way, which means that a large amount of functionality has to be deployed as a unit. Sometimes, as in our example, this can lead to massive dependencies even at the system level.

Disaggregating existing business processes and coming up with transition architectures (that accommodate the need to get work done while a partial solution is in place) can be quite difficult, as can MVP subsets of functionality that will deliver value on their own. Big bang release avoids those issues by simply pushing everything to one big event in the future.

Proposed solution

The big bang release anti-pattern proposes to just do one big release for all linked functionality at the end of a long delivery process. That can mean several years of work go-live at the same time without any intermediate feedback.

This solution can be highly attractive to both the delivery team and the customer for a variety of reasons:

- It reduces the entire system to a single deployment quantum that can be managed as a unit
- It simplifies the planning process as you don't have to plan for multiple releases, partial data migrations, and co-existence scenarios
- That means the overall architecture is also simplified as there is no need to come up with transition architectures for the scope of the project
- You also avoid tough decisions about what to include when and which business needs you can accommodate, and at what times
- It's easy to understand both for the delivery team and the customer
- You successfully push the problem down the line, making it something to deal with later. In some cases, there may even be other people doing it by then

You can, therefore, understand why—even at a time when small releases and DevOps thinking has become the leading paradigm—many projects still end up being deployed with a big bang. Unfortunately, it doesn't tend to go well.

Results

The fundamental problem with big bang releases is that you—often inadvertently—take on a massive amount of risk. Technical risk doesn't grow linearly with the number of components to deploy. Rather, it grows much faster due to the superlinear growth of interconnections and dependencies that come with a larger number of components.

Put simply, if you deploy one component, you only have the risk of that component failing to deal with. If you have just two interconnected components, you now have up to four failure modes to contend with:

- Component one failing independently

- Component two failing independently

- Component one failing and triggering a subsidiary failure in component two

- Component two failing and triggering a subsidiary failure in component one

All four may present unique symptoms and the root cause may not be obvious. Consider how many potential failure modes you'd have if you deployed 20 components together with a large number of interconnections between them.

Because the number of failure modes on a large deployment is so large, that necessarily means that testing becomes an enormous task, and often, you can test for weeks and still not be sure whether you have really tested all the important cases. Debugging errors is also much harder because tracing the potential knock-on effects between components is much harder than simply finding an error in a single component.

The same difficulties also apply to rolling out and rolling back any other cutover tasks that need to be done. Even training and change management becomes harder in a big-bang scenario.

Overall, the bigger the release, the more risk you have of it becoming a serious failure. Unless you are a gambler, you shouldn't go down that route.

Better solutions

If big releases are the problem, it stands to reason that small releases are the solution. From a risk management perspective, the ideal amount of functionality to release at a time is a single feature or a single user story. That is the premise of **continuous delivery** (**CD**), as practiced by leading DevOps-focused organizations.

However, we must acknowledge that not all organizations have the scale or technological sophistication to adopt the pure DevOps setup that would allow CD of a single feature at a time. However, if you aspire to the ideal of small releases, you will at least start to mitigate the problems.

Smaller releases have the following attributes:

- Less risky

- Easier to test

- Easier to debug

- Easier to fix errors in once found

- Easier to roll out and roll back

- Deliver value quicker to business users

- Facilitate and increase system adoption

- Make change management easier to control

Overall, once you do the necessary technical and business process work to enable smaller releases, there are few—if any—downsides.

Project pieism

Project pieism fails to contend with key architectural trade-offs, insisting instead that you can have your pie and eat it too.

Example

ConglomoCo is a large, diversified conglomerate that counts many **business units (BUs)**—some related to business lines, others to geography. Most BUs operate quite independently both operationally and with respect to IT infrastructure. In addition, BU heads have a lot of power relative to headquarters staff as they effectively are the masters of their own businesses.

When ConglomoCo's CIO decides to push for a global rollout of Salesforce, he is therefore met by staunch resistance on the part of several division heads that have their own CRM strategies and don't want HQ to get involved. However, as part of a new initiative, the CEO and CFO have requested a consolidated view of the global pipeline, which the CIO is leveraging for his Salesforce strategy.

Kim, a senior IT project manager with ConglomoCo's HQ staff, is therefore given the responsibility to drive the global rollout of Salesforce Sales Cloud and CPQ. The CIO wants to use this as an opportunity to standardize the core sales process across BUs and simplify the reporting of sales data.

After corresponding with his architects, Kim, therefore, proposes a plan based on a single org with a standard process. There will be local variations within the BUs, but these are to be kept limited in scope.

As Kim starts presenting this plan to stakeholders, he finds that it is clearly not what they were expecting. The BUs have separate processes, UX expectations, local integrations, and reporting needs that they are expecting a new system to cater to.

At a senior leader's workshop, many of these issues come to light, and a compromise is reached at the highest level. The new system must be able to cater to separate sales processes, automations, and local integrations and accommodate some level of customization of the UX for each BU:

Figure 7.2 – ConglomoCo org

However, all of this must still reside within the same Salesforce org and leverage the same data model to make reporting across BUs simpler. It is understood that this will lead to a more customized implementation and have a cost implication, but the CIO would still like the implementation to be as close to standard as possible.

The implementation is long and slow. By necessity, it includes many separate streams related to the different BUs. Every stream seems to have its own complexities, and coordinating between streams is an ongoing and uphill battle. It is fair to say that as the implementation goes on, a level of attrition sets in, and everybody lowers their expectations for the future system, seeing it more as a necessary evil than a driver of positive change.

Kim negotiates with the business and manages to get two of the smaller areas to go live in a pilot fashion. They go live without much fanfare and with a lot of bugs. Worse than the bugs, however, is the low adoption. The salespeople in the BUs seem to do everything possible to avoid putting data in the system, and when they do, it is of low quality.

Given the unpromising early results, the rest of the rollout is put on hold. Instead, a management consultancy is brought in to investigate why adoption is so poor and what could be done better going forward.

Problem

Project pieism is an anti-pattern that has its root cause in an aspiration to avoid having to make difficult trade-offs when implementing a system. That may be because of political difficulties or weak project leadership, but it always involves a failure to acknowledge a key trade-off that needs a decision.

In a sense, most engineering problems in software architecture and in general are about balancing a set of trade-offs. However, those trade-offs are often uncomfortable and will involve not pleasing all stakeholders.

Therefore, it's perfectly understandable that many projects proceed without making the necessary trade-offs in hope that a solution may be found later or simply by closing their eyes to the facts. In any case, it is an anti-pattern.

Proposed solution

Project pieism suggests as a solution to one or more important trade-offs in your solution that the trade-off is not real, that you don't really have to compromise, and that you can in fact have your pie and eat it too. Sometimes this is done by ignoring the trade-off or sweeping it under the rug; sometimes it is acknowledged but special pleading is deployed to suggest that this case is somehow special and therefore the trade-off does not apply.

This position is attractive for obvious reasons. When there are key trade-offs to be made in an implementation project, you will probably have to disappoint one or more groups of stakeholders. If those groups are powerful within your organization, that may not be an easy or pleasant thing to do. You can even find yourself in situations where you are forced into project pieism because of corporate politics.

However, not even the most powerful executive in your organization can change the basic facts of software architecture. There are always trade-offs. Whenever you have a situation on a technical project where there doesn't seem to be a trade-off in the decision you are making, you should be worried.

Results

The result of project pieism is the resurgence of the trade-off you've tried to ignore. Murphy's law being what it is, that will probably happen at the most inconvenient point in your project life cycle and cause major damage to your project.

Of course, the specific damage will depend on the trade-off you have been ignoring. In our preceding example, we ignored trade-offs between the priority of global and local processes and between the level of standard functionality versus customization.

ConglomoCo attempted to have a standard system with a global process that also accommodate all relevant local variations. That led to a system that no one wanted to use because it met no one's needs well enough.

Other trade-offs will have different consequences, but you can count on adverse consequences if you fail to make important decisions about the key trade-offs that drive your architecture.

Better solutions

The way to a less pieist future lies in openly acknowledging the trade-offs to be made and engaging constructively with stakeholders about the options. Often, there are ways of giving stakeholders more of what they all want, but it may come at an additional cost or a longer timeline.

One way to formalize this engagement is to set up good architectural governance early in a project and discuss the key architectural trade-offs in both architecture forums and business forums to ensure that all perspectives are taken into account. In our example, a competent architecture board might well have pointed out that there was no way of making a single org strategy work well in the ConglomoCo scenario.

As architects, we need to be honest with the business about what is and isn't possible. We are the people who know the art of the possible on the technical side, and we shouldn't pretend that our favorite technologies somehow transcend the need for making hard choices. Stand firm, be constructive, give options, and don't ignore important trade-offs.

Unpacking the pipeline

This section will introduce a key DevOps anti-pattern related to how you should structure your packages for package-based development.

Using packages to create silos

Using packages to create silos divides up the packages for your Salesforce project based on team structure without considering architectural concerns.

Example

MillCo, a producer of CNC milling machines with subsidiaries across Europe and North America, is implementing Salesforce for its B2B sales. This includes Sales Cloud, CPQ, and B2B Commerce.

Abigail is the CRM tech lead from MillCo, a role she has recently taken up after leading a CRM implementation project in another B2B manufacturing company. Her principal job is to ensure that the technical delivery from the three different vendors that are implementing the different elements of the new system is consistent and of high quality.

At project kick-off, Abigail invites all three vendor teams along with internal stakeholders and emphasizes many times that while people are working for different companies, everyone should think of themselves as being on the same team. MillCo wants everyone on the same page and working together toward a common goal.

That turns out to have been all for naught. Once work commences for real, the three suppliers are quickly at each other's throats. Abigail finds it impossible to get them to agree to any common approach and standard.

While she can mandate certain things, she has no team behind her, and there is only so much she can do if the vendors don't cooperate. She escalates the issue but is told to find a solution that allows work to continue as planned.

The solution she decides to go with is to isolate each vendor in a separate package. That way, they can build in isolation, excepting cases where their work directly clashes with one another on key elements of the platform. Abigail takes it upon herself to monitor and mediate these disputes:

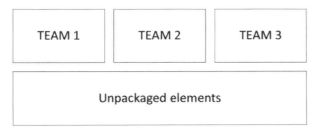

Figure 7.3 – Package structure

She ends up spending most of her time on the project mediating these kinds of inter-vendor conflicts. That also means she has very little time to investigate the general approaches used by the vendors in areas that aren't subject to acrimony.

However, in the end, the system is built. As each vendor has been working in their own environment with only occasional deploys to a thinly tested integration environment, the first step to prepare for **user acceptance testing** (**UAT**) is to deploy all the packages to a common environment and test the basic processes. Each package has been thoroughly tested in its own environment, but no systematic testing has been done across packages.

Even before the test results start coming in, the situation starts to deteriorate. It turns out that there are incompatible system and package settings between the vendors—for instance, on the CPQ-managed package. This means the deployment stalls until a workaround can be found.

When the testers actually get started, things go from bad to worse. There are many subtle incompatibilities between the packages. For instance, there are different interpretations and uses of common fields, duplicate fields used by different packages for the same purpose, and custom objects that have a partially overlapping scope and the creation of redundant data. There is also a wide range of different automation patterns in use between the three vendors, despite this being an area where Abigail specified the standard upfront.

All in all, the differences are too large to reconcile quickly, and the project has to back off. Abigail's boss negotiates an extension to the timeline in order to refactor the packages and bring them in line. While she is happy about the extension, Abigail does not relish the wrangling it will take to get the vendors to actually do this.

Problem

Sometimes, you want to allow teams to work independently without having to depend on or coordinate with other teams. In a Salesforce context, that may be because the teams are working on different clouds, come from different vendors, or represent different departments or BUs within your organization.

This is very understandable as coordination problems can be hard to resolve. However, when that becomes the basis for dividing up your Salesforce platform into packages, it becomes a DevOps anti-pattern.

Proposed solution

The proposed solution of using packages to create silos is to give each team its own package to work in, reflecting what it is going to be working on. That avoids coordination issues but creates a host of other problems.

That means you structure the package setup for your project based on organizational needs rather than architecture. That can seem like a good idea at the outset and obviously works for the teams in the short term, but unfortunately means that hidden conflicts are likely and can remain hidden for a long time.

Results

The likely result of Using packages to create silos is that you will have hidden conflicts that only become apparent on the integration of the packages.

These conflicts include cases such as the following:

- Different use of data models—for instance, fields and objects
- Issues in security model where conflicting configurations are used
- Conflicting flows, validation rules, or other business logic
- Deviation from best practice, for instance multiple triggers on same object
- Different automation patterns used on the same object
- Conflicting assumptions about system settings
- Replicated functionality in different packages that is often only partially overlapping

This can lead to serious issues and can be a real mess to refactor, which is both costly and time-consuming.

Better solutions

In general, package design should be taken quite seriously. Package-based development is the direction of travel for most large-scale Salesforce projects, not least because it scales better than the alternatives.

To avoid falling into the using packages to create silos anti-pattern, follow these guidelines:

- Design your package structure with your architecture in mind. For instance, in a typical architecture that's split by service lines, you could place common functionality in a "Common" package that all other packages depend on and then have separate packages for each service line containing relevant components. You might also have higher-level packages cutting across service lines for things such as common integrations and you could have separate packages split out for cross-cutting functionality, although that can be a bit tricky to manage. The point is that you should ensure that you manage dependencies cleanly and don't have potentially conflicting overlaps.

- Be careful with dependencies; a layered approach can work well to only have dependencies go in one direction.

- Have teams work across packages when needed.

- Consider having certain teams own certain packages and others request work from them if they need anything.

- Coordinate via technical governance forums—for example, an architecture board.

In general, you don't want to mistake package design for something else. Build your package structure so that it makes sense for your architecture and is workable for your developers.

Testing without testing

Testing is a critical activity within any large software project. In this section, we will see how trying to avoid writing the necessary unit tests can cause major issues in the mid-to-long term.

Dummy unit tests

The dummy unit tests anti-pattern gets around the built-in requirement for unit testing in Salesforce by writing dummy tests that optimize for coverage but do nothing.

Example

TruckCo is a start-up automotive company that focuses on building next-generation EV trucks. It sees itself as more of a technology company than a manufacturing company and therefore invests heavily in top-range solutions to keep its technological edge.

Generally, TruckCo tends toward heavy customization and intense agile projects with long hours and short timelines. The supply chain application TruckCo is currently building on Salesforce is no exception to this rule.

The application will integrate their B2B commerce portal with order management and their supply chain backend systems. It will enable **just-in-time** (**JIT**) ordering from spare parts vendors and in general significantly reduce the **quote-to-cash** (**QTC**) process for spare part orders.

In order to achieve these aims, TruckCo plans to integrate half a dozen key backend systems with Salesforce, build a custom **user interface** (**UI**) optimized for their special processes, and build a set of cross-platform, AI-enabled automations that drive efficiencies in the ordering process.

Because the application is expected to be code-heavy and development-focused, TruckCo repurposes a team of Java developers from its permanent staff to work on it, figuring that Apex is close enough for them to pick it up as they go along. Yana is the only traditional Salesforce person on the project, and her role is to guide the rest of the team in the ways of Salesforce.

Matt, the team lead, is a bit of a maverick, and the same is true of the rest of the team. While they use unit tests, they do not do so consistently, often preferring to have bugs reported by users and then fix them afterward. Inside TruckCo, there is an unstated but strong preference for releasing products on time, even if that means releasing something buggy and incomplete.

Coming from the Java world, the developers quickly start to get annoyed with the mandated 75% unit test coverage enforced by Salesforce and built into the deployment tooling for the platform. Yana accidentally mentions some ways to fool the Salesforce unit test calculation by creating dummy tests while having lunch with the rest of the team.

Although she mentioned it jokingly, much to her chagrin, she finds that a few days after, dummy unit tests are starting to appear in the code base. When she calls out Matt on this, he simply shrugs and says that they're behind schedule, so they don't have time to spend all their time coding tests.

Yana, however, is not deterred, and at the next project board, she raises the issue formally. She refers to the guidance provided by Salesforce and supported by the company's own Salesforce architect.

The project sponsor promises to have someone investigate the issue. Unfortunately, that's the last Yana hears of it. It seems that Matt had indicated that major delays would happen to the project if they had to retroactively write a complete set of unit tests. In keeping with TruckCo's normal way of operating, this is seen as unacceptable, and the dummy unit test issue is ignored.

Therefore, the practice keeps accelerating as the project falls more behind, and toward go-live, almost every new unit test written is a dummy. While the automated scanner lists an impressive 90% coverage, Yana doubts if the real number is any higher than 10%.

A few weeks before go-live, a list of last-minute changes comes in from business stakeholders. Yana can't see any way that they can be incorporated, but Matt agrees to deliver them.

The last period is a flurry of changes back and forth with lots of bugs discovered by testers, followed by fixes that often lead to further regression issues. This continues unabated into the actual UAT period, which finds another large number of issues. However, no one takes the decision to halt the go-live, and on the appointed day, the supply chain application goes live.

As users start onboarding on the application, several breaking bugs are discovered in the main flows. These occurred in areas that had been tested and found working just weeks before go-live and had also been part of user training.

The application must be taken down, and an escalation meeting is called. Here, the fundamental soundness and quality of the application are put into serious question and a new initiative is agreed upon to look into the quality issues and devise a way of fixing them before the application can be brought back online.

Problem

Dummy unit tests seek to address a very simple question: how do you get around the hard 75% unit test limit for production deployment in Salesforce? It's common for long-running Salesforce projects to find that they are under the limit either for a specific deployment or in general.

Many teams find this limit annoying. This is especially true, when developers are coming to the platform from other technologies where no such limit existed or when under pressure, or when they are doing something "simple".

Proposed solution

The solution proposed is to create dummy unit tests that just optimize for code coverage and don't really test anything. This is another of the few anti-patterns that edge close to just being bad practice. You can see an example of a dummy test in the following code snippet:

```
@isTest
class dummyTest{
```

```
static testMethod void notRealTest(){
   //assume A is a class with two methods
   A aInstance = new A();
   aInstance.methodA();
   aInstance.methodB();
   //nothing is done to test anything
}
}
```

However, it is something that can be tempting and that otherwise serious Salesforce practitioners sometimes may engage in. When you are under pressure to meet a sprint goal or deployment deadline, it can seem like a waste of time to write a bunch of unit tests just to get the coverage up.

But obviously, this attitude fails to acknowledge the real value provided by unit tests and the reason why the coverage is mandatory: code without good unit tests is much more brittle and prone to regression errors than code that has them. Therefore, skipping them, even when you are under pressure, is a genuinely bad idea.

Results

This pattern tends to lead to death of a thousand cuts. While you probably don't experience ill effects in the short term, after a while you don't have any real unit tests to rely on.

Even worse, you may still psychologically project a false sense of security, if you still think you've only cut the corners in a few places and generally can rely on your testing. Basically, you are cheating the system and probably releasing poor-quality code. Also, you are creating a major amount of technical debt that the organization will at some point have to pay off.

Better solutions

The solution to this anti-pattern is simple: build good unit tests and meet the minimum thresholds, always. You should never compromise on the minimum bar as it will lead to deteriorating code quality and hence delivery quality over time.

There is a lot of guidance available on building good unit tests, so let us just rehearse a few basic points:

- A unit test should test a single functionality in the code
- The test should be written before the code it is testing
- The test should be written in such a way that it can be easily repeated
- The test should be independent of other tests
- The test should not rely on org data but should create its own test data, ideally using a test data factory

- The test should be concise

- Assertions should be used to check that the expected results are obtained

- The test should test both positive and negative cases

- The test should be run often, preferably automatically

- The test should be easy to understand and maintain

It is a rare anti-pattern that can be avoided just by following good practice, so be sure to avoid this one.

Knowing the takeaways

In this section, we will abstract a bit from the specific patterns and instead try to pull out the wider learning points you can use in your day-to-day work as a Salesforce architect or in preparing for the CTA Review Board.

When architecting Salesforce solutions, you should be mindful of the following:

- Don't put all your eggs in one basket. Plan smaller releases wherever possible to de-risk and get feedback.

- Confront the tough decisions that can come from having to break down functionality into smaller buckets. Don't just accept a statement that everything must be there from day one.

- Always confront the key architectural trade-offs early on in your project timeline. They usually don't get easier to manage as time goes by.

- Communicate clearly and openly about the trade-offs that need to be made and the options for doing so. Trying to please everybody and sweep things under the rug is a recipe for disaster.

- Don't allow team rivalries or organizational silos to dictate your development model, whether for package-based development or otherwise.

- Instead, ensure that your development model is consistent with the architecture you are pursuing and that components and packages are structured accordingly.

- Unit testing is a requirement in Salesforce for a reason. Don't compromise just because you are under pressure.

- Writing good-quality unit tests will ensure that you have higher code quality and fewer regression issues.

In preparing for the CTA Review Board, you should be mindful of the following:

- Prefer an agile, multi-release process when faced with a big complex scenario, rather than a single big-bang release.

- Some scenarios, however, do seem written more toward a waterfall/big-bang approach. This may be an area where best practices for the board and for reality can diverge.

- You should be very clear about the trade-offs you are making and include them in your justification.

- If you fail to make an appropriate choice, it will with near certainty make your solution unravel during Q&A.

- Package-based development is the up-and-coming development model for Salesforce projects, but that doesn't mean it will be right for your scenario.

- If it is, having some words to say about a good package structure will potentially give you some extra kudos.

- Know the minimum limits for unit testing and when they are applied so that you can answer if asked.

- Also, be prepared to answer general questions about what makes good unit tests and how to use them to improve code quality.

We have now covered the material for this chapter and are ready to proceed. First, however, we will summarize our learning.

Summary

In this chapter, we have seen examples of how the development life cycle can be impacted by anti-patterns at different levels of abstraction. At the highest level, how you deal with key trade-offs and how you structure your releases have a huge impact on the potential success of your project.

However, we also saw that technical elements such as how your structure your packages and whether you write good unit tests can be major contributors to project success or failure. That means you must master all of these levels to be a successful architect in this domain.

For many architects, this domain can be a bit of a lower priority relative to solution architecture or the hardcore technical domains. However, paying insufficient attention to these issues can lead to serious project failures just as easily as a badly designed solution.

With that being said, we will now continue to our last domain—namely, communication—and see how we can mess up our Salesforce projects by communicating in the wrong way.

8

Communication
without Mistranslation

This final chapter before the conclusion will deal with anti-patterns centered around the way you communicate architecture to different audiences. The first part describes an anti-pattern related to information control. Then we look at a few anti-patterns that relate to the clarity of your communication. Third, we look at an anti-pattern specifically concerning the way you create architectural artifacts. As we've been doing all along, we will end the chapter by summarizing our key takeaways.

In this chapter, we're going to cover the following main topics:

- How overcommunication can in some cases be worse than undercommunication, especially when communicating with a generalist audience

- How keeping things ambiguous in order to avoid making a decision can result in serious damage to your project

- How people's seeming inability to understand what you are saying is often a symptom of underlying issues you need to address

- Why straying from standards when documenting technical specifications is almost always a bad idea

After completing this chapter, you will have a better understanding of how technical communication can go wrong. More importantly, you will have picked up a number of concrete approaches you can apply to help you avoid common technical communication pitfalls.

Communicating too much

This section will explore what happens when you communicate too much in a technical context. To do this, we will start by exploring an anti-pattern taken straight out of cognitive psychology: cognitive overload.

Cognitive overload

Cognitive overload happens when the amount of information presented becomes overwhelming to the recipient to the extent that it impairs action.

Example

LilacCo, the world's leading producer of scented candles, is having major issues with its integration landscape. It has a relatively recently purchased MuleSoft platform, but it has seen little use, and most integrations still run through legacy middleware or point-to-point.

Martin is a technical architect who has been given the task to come up with a solution to the various issues LilacCo is experiencing. The issues include high latency and slow performance on many integrations, poor logging and monitoring, long and error-prone development cycles, and the inability to create new integrations for several key legacy systems.

Martin has thought long and hard about the issue and has come to the conclusion that moving more systematically to MuleSoft, implementing more event-driven and asynchronous integrations, writing some key adaptor APIs in front of older legacy systems, and providing a clear pattern for error handling and logging to be used by all teams will solve the problem.

It is not an easy fix. Martin has created a slide deck and accompanying report numbering hundreds of pages. The material contains many technical diagrams, and although he has tried to create appropriate summaries, he feels that there is only so far this material can be simplified without losing the essence of what is being said.

Martin pitches his new model to the executive board. Unfortunately, the questions asked reveal that no one has really understood the message he has tried to convey. They get hung up on relatively insignificant details and fail to grasp the overall plan.

He is given feedback that his proposed model is too complex and that he needs to find a simpler approach. Martin is exasperated. He already felt like the plan he had come up with was the simplest possible. The elements all rely on each other, and removing any would compromise the approach.

Martin tries to schedule one-to-one conversations with the people he knows best on the executive board in order to rerun his key points by them. Even in this more intimate context, Martin finds it difficult to bring his points across. The key points simply seem to get lost in translation.

Then, Martin is told that a new integration platform vendor has had a pitch in front of the executive board and that everyone is very excited about the new approach they are bringing. Martin is asked to give feedback, which he does in the form of a detailed and nuanced rebuttal of the vendor pitch. He concludes that while the new platform indeed has some exciting features, it does not solve the fundamental problems LilacCo is facing.

Martin's feedback, however, accomplishes very little. The vendor proposes to do a free **proof of concept** (**POC**) to create more comfort in their software's capabilities, which the executive board accepts. Martin is not asked to be part of the POC team.

6 weeks later, the POC concludes with roaring success. The team has been able to demonstrate all the capabilities required during this period. Of course, it's all on a pilot basis and much complexity remains, but the executive board is confident based on the presentation it receives from the team that the new software will deliver what it needs.

Martin asks whether he can look into the details of the POC and what has actually been demonstrated, but his request is silently ignored. Instead, the vendor sends a formal proposal, which is accepted, and a new project to implement the new integration platform is underway.

Problem

Cognitive overload is a general term from psychology for situations where our brains are overloaded with information or options to the point where we are unable to take the required actions that we would normally be able to in the presence of less information. In technical communication, creating cognitive overload by including too much information when presenting architectural options is a very common anti-pattern.

This especially happens when we convey information to non-technical audiences. For technical audiences, we can to a large extent rely on an understanding of diagram formats, standard ways of doing things, good practice, architecture patterns, and similar.

That reduces the cognitive complexity for such an audience, although complex architectures can still be hard to follow even for experienced practitioners. However, when you are trying to convey this information to a general audience, you cannot rely on these supports, and therefore the task of conveying key trade-offs and many moving parts can be extremely difficult.

Proposed solution

Cognitive overload isn't a solution per se. What leads to cognitive overload is the belief that you, somehow, need to include a certain amount of detail in your presentation in order to be fair to your audience or complete in relation to your subject.

My personal belief is that a large number of talented architects fall into this anti-pattern because of a sense of intellectual honesty. They have considered many options and are aware of many arguments and counterarguments for and against the solution they are proposing.

Therefore, they feel dishonest in simply doubling down on a highly simplified version of the option they have chosen to recommend. In scenarios where business stakeholders are the ultimate decision-makers, which is often the case even for seemingly architectural decisions, that almost inevitably leads to cognitive overload.

Results

The obvious result is a failure of communication. Your main recommendation and supporting points are lost in a quagmire of information that your audience is unable to process.

That means you lose your audience and their attention and, ultimately, your ability to influence them to make the decision you want them to make. Cognitive overload leads to inaction, so the most likely result is that nothing will come out of what you are proposing because it has not been assimilated.

That also leaves the field open for other players to sell a different message, as we saw in our example. It is an unfortunate fact in our industry that it is often the most well-placed messaging that leads to technology adoption rather than the optimal choice from a technical point of view.

Better solutions

Effective communication is not something that can be taught in a few sentences. But your takeaway should be that it is important to simplify a complex message sufficiently for it to be understandable for your audience.

In general, stick to the following:

- Structure the message for the audience and their level of understanding
- Don't assume the audience know even the basics of what you are proposing unless you know for a fact that they do
- Focus on a single main message; don't include lots of subsidiary messages alongside the main one
- Don't include all additional considerations and options you have considered along the way.
- Use images, graphics, tables, and so on to help get information across
- Have backup material ready if anyone wants to dive deeper into an area, but don't include it upfront

Overall, you should be cautious about making demands on your audience. They have a lot on their plate and limited time to engage with what you have to say. Make sure that time counts.

Being unclear in several ways

In this section, we explore two anti-patterns that in different ways explore intentional and unintentional lack of clarity in technical communication. We start by exploring an anti-pattern that seeks to deploy a lack of clarity for a tactical purpose but ends up causing adverse effects.

Ambiguous solution

Ambiguous solution proposes to hide away a conflicted or uncertain decision
behind ambiguous language and representations to postpone the need to make it.

Example

GrillCo, a major online retailer focused on outdoor cooking equipment, is facing major issues in its order management process. There are frequent unanticipated stock-outs, wrong delivery calculations both for duration and costs, and taxes are not consistently applied correctly.

This is not entirely an IT problem, and in fact, many areas of process improvement have been identified. However, as part of the wider order management transformation, GrillCo management has also decided that it needs a new software platform for the order management process.

There are, however, several opinions as to which software to get and how to go about implementing it. Some support putting it in the Salesforce CRM, using the out-of-the-box order management module. Others would prefer dealing with a dedicated vendor with a more retail-focused attitude. Finally, IT would prefer implementing the functionality themselves, using the microservices architecture they have been building up.

Rainer has the technical project management responsibility for the order management implementation. He tries to facilitate the discussion between the different proposals, but the problem is that nobody seems to know who should be making the decision.

In the meantime, there are many other smaller technical tasks to get on with, so Rainer focuses on these, leaving the new order management system as a generic capability on diagrams, presentations, and documentation. He figures that a solution will be arrived at eventually, so there is no need to rock the boat.

However, as the transformation proceeds on other fronts, the question becomes more urgent in the minds of the senior stakeholders. As he has been unable to gain consensus by talking to people, he proposes to do a formal vendor selection with well-defined criteria and let that be the decision-making process.

However, as he starts to prepare the groundwork for the selection process, he makes a startling discovery. Two teams have separately gone ahead with completely different pilot implementations of the order management software based on their own interpretation of requirements:

- The first is within the IT department, where a few developers have started prototyping new software to show how flexible and powerful their microservices platform is. While it has some good functionality, it does not in Rainer's assessment begin to meet the real needs of the business.

- The second pilot is even further along, already working with mock ordering scenarios based on data taken from the existing e-commerce solution. It is based on a piece of standard software from a small retail-focused software vendor that is investing heavily in making the necessary adaptations to meet GrillCo's needs. However, Rainer again assesses that there is much to be done before this solution might be fit for purpose.

A dramatic meeting ensues with the CIO and the IT team on one side and the COO and the supply chain team on the other, both championing one of the solutions. The meeting ends as a stalemate, and a decision is made to bring in an independent consultant to assess the two solutions and make a recommendation.

GrillCo brings in a high-profile and well-respected expert in order management solutions who spends a few weeks looking at the pilot software. His assessment is damning.

Neither pilot really has a good way of delivering the level of capability GrillCo needs. He recommends proceeding with neither solution and instead going back to the market to find a better fit. Rainer polishes his presentation on the technology vendor selection process and gets to work.

Problem

Some decisions are hard to make. This can be because of politics—that is to say, not wanting to annoy powerful stakeholders or groups with a decision they won't like. It can also be due to missing information that will only appear at a later stage in the process and therefore complicates making a decision now.

The art of avoiding a controversial decision by postponing it is the core of the problem addressed by the ambiguous solution anti-pattern. While it can be reasonable to take some time to collect more specific information that will significantly increase decision quality, taking this too far becomes an anti-pattern, no matter if it is done due to politics or a general fear of getting the decision wrong.

Proposed solution

The ambiguous solution anti-pattern proposes to handle difficult decisions by hiding them behind ambiguity. This can easily be done through things such as capability models, by deferring to a separate decision process, or by simply listing multiple alternatives—for instance, in diagrams and documentation.

This can be a highly attractive option in a number of cases; for instance, you may know that certain very senior stakeholders favor a certain approach that you have determined to be unviable. By hiding behind ambiguity, you may hope to postpone making this clear until the project is too far along to change things.

You may also, secretly, be hoping that as the project progresses and more information becomes available, the decision will become easier; either it will be too late to activate some options or the answer will become obvious.

That is to say, you are hoping not to have to handle a situation that has a high degree of uncertainty or conflict attached to it by postponing it indefinitely. This is very human behavior, but, unfortunately, is a bad architectural practice.

Results

Ultimately, of course, you will need to deal with the issue you have been hiding away. If you are lucky, the decision will now be easy as most avenues will be foreclosed. This is not a good thing, however.

It will rarely be the case that the option that can be implemented most swiftly is also the optimal solution. Therefore, your procrastination in dealing with the issue will nearly always result in a worse solution than if you had made the decision sooner.

There is something to be said for keeping options open when the decision isn't necessary, but if you do it for too long, it will adversely affect your solution. And keeping options open for too long when it comes to key architectural decisions is generally problematic.

If you aren't lucky, the decision still won't be obvious; you still must deal with uncertainty and conflict, but now it will be compounded by the additional time pressure you have added by waiting. This is altogether a worse outcome both for you personally and for the project.

Better solutions

First, don't postpone a decision beyond its last sell-by date. If you don't have the necessary information, make a plan with a clear deadline for getting it together. Then, plan a decision-making process that will take place at that time whatever else happens.

If the decision is politically unpalatable, try to get your supporters within the organization to stand by you as you make and communicate it. There's always a risk of the wrong decision being made for political reasons.

However, even the wrong decision is better than no decision after a point. At least you will be making progress and you will be able to start mitigating the consequences of a wrong decision sooner.

When decisions are needed, flag them clearly in documentation and presentations so that stakeholders are aware the decision is coming. Don't hide behind vagueness, even when it's easy to do so.

If you can't decide by consensus, see if you can get stakeholders to agree on a formal decision-making process instead. Often, people find it easier to live with the outcome of a formal process than with something that appears as just some guy's opinion.

Groundhog day

The groundhog day anti-pattern happens when people endlessly ask the same questions, even after multiple repeated explanations.

Example

Rolf is leading a local Salesforce implementation for MediCo, a medical device manufacturer with a presence in most European markets. The Salesforce implementation has been defined by the HQ staff in Paris and is meant to be rolled out as is to the various subsidiaries in other countries.

Rolf has been given the responsibility to roll out the system to the German subsidiary. The German operation is new to MediCo, having only been acquired the previous year. It, therefore, is not tightly integrated into MediCo's standard processes or IT infrastructure. The Salesforce implementation is seen as a way to improve upon this state of affairs.

When he delivers the initial presentation on the Salesforce implementation as it exists in France and other countries to the German team, he is met with a barrage of questions. The team wants to drill into very specific process questions that Rolf has no way of answering, as he doesn't know the details of the German operation.

He takes away a ton of questions, which he tries his best to answer in written format. However, he quickly starts feeling like he is playing a game of whack-a-mole. Every time he seemingly answers a question, another similar but subtly different question pops up from another member of staff.

Rolf starts consolidating all the questions and prepares clear and concise answers to all of them. Given the high degree of confusion, he has not been able to make any real progress with the implementation, so he decides to give it one more go.

He gathers the German team together one more time to give the team members the highlights of the new Salesforce system and as systematically as possible to address all the concerns that have been raised so far. To no avail, he is once again met with more uncomprehending glances and questions that he thought he had already answered more than once.

Frustrated and almost ready to give up, Rolf decides to call one of his old mentors in the company, who he knows is aware of the situation in the German subsidiary. She tells Rolf that the problem is probably not with his communication skills at all.

The staff in the German subsidiary prefer to do things their own way and resent the imposition from HQ. Salesforce is just a pretense for voicing that opposition. The system could be the most perfect thing since sliced bread, but the German team would still oppose it out of principle.

With his new knowledge, Rolf decides on a new plan. He takes the bold decision to put things out in the open. He holds another presentation, where he makes it clear that he is aware of the real reason for the opposition, and rather than trying to address all the concerns, he invites the team into the process to see how it might find a way of making the new system its own.

While the system is what it is and HQ is not about to approve a lot of local changes, how the German operation decides to adopt it and integrate it into its own processes is up for grabs. Rolf opens up the implementation to the German team and welcomes its suggestions for how it might best use the new

CRM. Slowly, some people start to engage, and while the timeline has to be moved a couple of times, eventually adoption is successful.

Problem

Sometimes, people just don't seem to understand what you're saying. No matter how hard you try to explain a point or how many times you explain it, there doesn't seem to be any getting your point across.

The groundhog day anti-pattern, named after the movie of the same name, describes this situation where you can't seemingly communicate something enough times for it to make any difference.

That means you feel like you are banging your head against a wall without making the slightest mark. Often, this is because you aren't really engaging with the underlying issues that are in play.

Proposed solution

When you engage in the groundhog day anti-pattern, you respond to the situation of having seemingly never-ending queries about the same issues by repeating yourself a lot. You may repeat yourself in different languages or in different modalities, but you are reiterating the same message.

Sometimes, it can make life feel like an endless repetition and like you are making no progress at all. You question both your own sanity and the sanity of the people doing the continuous questioning.

That's generally because you are not really engaging the underlying reason for why the questions are asked. Generally, when you are asked the same thing more than a couple of times by the same people, some kind of resistance is at play.

Maybe, the people feel like a bad decision has been made over their heads and they are trying to pick it apart. Maybe they are anxious that the direction you are proposing will lead to bad personal consequences for them.

There are many reasons people might have to resist your message that have nothing to do with how you present or communicate that message. In this case, the problem becomes more about change management than about communication, and being aware enough to catch this phenomenon is a key soft skill to acquire if you are a practicing architect.

Results

The results of the groundhog day anti-pattern are substantially negative both on a personal level and for your project:

- First of all, you get nowhere with the message you are trying to communicate, which usually needs to be accepted by the audience to which you are communicating

- That leaves you frustrated as you ponder how to better communicate your message to the audience and continuously fail

- It leaves the people you are communicating with frustrated as they don't feel you are listening to their real concerns

- The project, in the meanwhile, usually stalls, and progress on key areas can be blocked due to the communication impasse

Overall, this anti-pattern can be a serious strain on your project and on you.

Better solutions

The first step is to recognize that the problem exists and is not about you finding a better way of saying the same thing.

In general, remember the following:

- Once you begin hearing the same questions over and over again in slightly different variations, pause and take a step back

- Engage with stakeholders and allies to figure out what are the real reasons behind the resistance that you are facing

- If you find that there are reasons that lie behind the consistent questioning that go beyond just comprehension, work actively to find an alternative approach without compromising your core goals

- Then, apply good change management practices to help drive the needed transformation

You can't always give people what they want, but you can find a way of acknowledging their real concerns and being open to their feedback.

Drawing diagrams with excess creativity

This section explores what happens when you try to communicate technical information with too much creativity rather than relying on established practice within your community. We do this by looking at the non-standard documentation anti-pattern.

Non-standard documentation

Non-standard documentation refers to an anti-pattern, where teams produce technical documentation in an idiosyncratic format rather than relying on standard practice.

Example

SafeCo, the leading provider of security solutions for facility management, is in the visioning phase of a new Salesforce implementation. It is trying to come up with a strategy for completely transforming its business using technology and has bought into Salesforce as part of the solution.

Qin, a strategy manager with SafeCo, is leading the visioning exercise and is supported by an external consultancy with particular strength in design thinking. They run a series of highly engaging workshops that result in a vision and key requirements for the new strategic technology platform.

The outputs of the workshop are documented in a fairly large number of rich pictures and ad hoc diagrams, many combining elements of process design, data models, and UX prototypes. The senior managers who have been part of the workshop like the outputs so much that they decide to include them in the **Request for Proposals (RFP)** material that will be sent to potential vendors.

SafeCo shortlists three vendors that all make explicit reference to the workshop outputs in their RFP responses. After final presentations, SafeCo selects one of the largest global Salesforce partners to carry out its implementation in line with requirements as principally stated by the workshop outputs.

However, once the vendor has mobilized and the project enters a formal discovery phase, it becomes clear that there are problems. Many features and requirements that SafeCo thought were obvious from the provided documents have not been included in the vendor's estimates.

SafeCo pushes hard on the vendor, pointing to the documentation provided with the RFP. However, the vendor disputes the interpretation of the documentation, and it proves impossible to demonstrate clear intent for many of the points under dispute.

For a moment, SafeCo considers going back to market, but the vendor was selected as the only one that had the necessary mix of competencies available on the timeline it needed. Senior management is not willing to compromise on the project deadline and so redoing the procurement doesn't seem feasible.

Therefore, the only thing to do is to negotiate an agreement for additional features that the vendor had not included. After some amount of wrangling, a compromise is reached that leaves neither party fully satisfied.

The price of the project goes up but not by as much as the vendor wanted. In addition, the vendor insists on more formal documentation of the requirements to be implemented during the project, taking away some of the flexibility that was part of the initial plan. With the compromise in place, the project can finally commence.

Problem

The problem addressed by the non-standard documentation anti-pattern is how to best communicate complex requirements, architectures, designs, and general expectations of technical systems. This touches on the differences between communicating general concepts to a generalist audience versus communicating technical concepts to a technical audience.

Generally, highly visual and engaging material tends to play well when in a workshop setting, such as defining the vision for a new system or how to use an enterprise software platform such as Salesforce for strategic advantage. In this case, you want to use formats that resonate with your audience and build a common understanding.

However, this approach can lead you into trouble when communication needs to be precise and technically correct.

Proposed solution

Non-standard documentation proposes that the best documentation is the one clearest to the key stakeholders involved in producing it, whatever that might be. This is an extremely seductive position because it is true in many cases.

For instance, it is true in the following cases:

- If you are trying to gain alignment about a vision or project
- If you are trying to foster mutual understanding within an organization about a certain topic
- If you are trying to create general awareness of an issue

In all these cases, the perfect documentation is the one that works well for the audience. However, when it comes to technical specifications, architectures, and designs, this ceases to be the case.

Results

Normal language tolerates a lot of ambiguity. The same is true of most visual representations of concepts. However, ambiguity is the mortal enemy of technical specification.

To reduce the amount of ambiguity when writing technical specifications, whether of requirements, architectures, designs, or in general, we use a number of tools. These include the following:

- Language that is stripped of everyday niceties and strives consistently for clarity
- Referring to technical standards that have a well-defined common understanding
- Referring to patterns that are common within our technical community and likely to be readily understood by the recipients of our communication
- Referring to conventions or common ways of doing things that are common within our technical community and likely to be readily understood by the recipients of our communication
- Using standard formats for documentation that have a structure sure to address the common concerns expected by members of our technical community
- Using standard formats for diagrams that are well understood by members of our technical community

All these elements help to reduce the ambiguity of technical specifications, although even with all of these in play, there is still plenty of scope for misunderstanding, as any experienced architect will tell you.

That is why there are standard ways such as user stories or a traditional requirements specification to convey requirements, and standard diagram types such as system landscapes, process diagrams, and data models to convey technical design.

If you stray from these standards, you add to the total ambiguity, and that will cause communication trouble, which can be expensive as your vendors or staff will not understand precisely what is needed. There is enough trouble with communication even with precisely defined requirements and design—don't add to it.

Better solutions

Given the description in the previous section, it's probably not difficult to surmise what you should do instead. Let us list them for good measure:

- Write your technical specifications with a view to reducing ambiguity. Strive for clarity above all else.

- Rely as much as possible on standard diagram types, ways of presenting material, naming, and so on whenever you are creating a technical specification that needs to be shared.

- Follow the patterns and conventions common within your technical community. For Salesforce professionals, this generally means following the approach that Salesforce itself uses.

That way, you can communicate clearly with vendors and new technical people that you hire, avoiding the parts of ambiguity that are avoidable.

Remember—in contrast with most communication where you are trying to make a general point, with technical communication you are trying to make an exact one. That is a very hard thing to do, as it turns out.

For Salesforce, specifically, the *Salesforce Architects* website, `https://architect.salesforce.com/diagrams`, will help you get a good overview of resources shared by Salesforce itself now available to all architects to avoid re-inventing the wheel when documenting and presenting Salesforce solutions. For readers interested in preparing for the CTA board, this is a great place to keep in mind.

Now, having covered the patterns for this chapter, let us proceed to discuss the key takeaways.

Knowing the takeaways

In this section, we will abstract a bit from the specific patterns and instead try to pull out the wider learning points you can use in your day-to-day work as a Salesforce architect or in preparing for the CTA Review Board.

When architecting Salesforce solutions, you should be mindful of the following:

- Don't include too much information when presenting your architecture to business stakeholders.

- Instead, focus on your main message and include only essential supporting information.

- Don't feel bad about not including all the additional considerations you had in coming up with your solution. If anybody wants more detail, they can ask for it afterward.

- Don't postpone decisions beyond the latest point it makes sense to take them, even if making a decision is hard.

- If a decision is controversial or politically sensitive, deferring to a formal decision process can provide a way forward.

- If you have a situation where it seems like you can't get your audience to understand you, you should start suspecting that there are some underlying sources of resistance.

- In that case, you will most likely need to focus on the change management aspects of the situation before you can make real progress.

- When it comes time to prepare documentation for a technical audience, whether an external audience or your internal technical teams, you should be rigorous about sticking to accepted practice within your technical community.

- For Salesforce professionals, that generally means adopting the practices disseminated by Salesforce itself.

In preparing for the CTA Review Board, you should be mindful of the following:

- Be short and crisp when presenting your solutions. The judges are experienced architects, so you can rely on a lot of background knowledge.

- Include a clear justification of your recommendations but do not dwell on alternatives.

- Don't include additional considerations that are not essential to your main point. If anybody wants to test your thinking, they will do so in the Q&A.

- Ambiguity is nobody's friend. Don't present solutions that aren't clear or fail to make important architectural decisions.

- The judges are highly experienced in ferreting out areas where you are missing clarity, so if you aren't sure what the right decision is, you should make one anyways.

- If the judges ask the same or nearly the same question multiple times, they are probably hinting at an area of weakness in your solution that you may want to reconsider on the fly.

- Use the standard diagrams and presentation formats that have been successful for previous CTA candidates.

- Do things the same way repeatedly in your mock exams to develop facility and speed.

We have now covered the material for this chapter and are ready to proceed. First, however, we will summarize our learning.

Summary

In this chapter, we have seen how communication can seriously affect the outcomes of our projects. You can have the best architecture in the world and it can still fail to make any headway if you fail to communicate it properly or fail to deal with the resistance it engenders in your target audience.

This can be dispiriting to some architects of a more rationalistic bend. Surely, the facts and substance should be the determining factors. Unfortunately, in most organizations, better communication skills will beat stronger technical architecture skills in terms of getting things done.

The good thing is that communication skills, as with all skills, can be learned. There isn't anything particularly hard about the ways in which you need to communicate to have greater success as an architect—it is just something that takes some practice.

We have now covered all the subject matter of the book and are ready to proceed to the conclusion, where we will summarize the journey we've been on together and look at where to go from here.

9
Conclusion

This conclusion gives a broad overview of the content of the book, including the overarching takeaways from the preceding chapters. It then explains how you can use the anti-pattern method and perspective in your own work to improve your architecture skills. Finally, it gives you pointers on how you can go to progress further in this direction.

In this chapter, we're going to cover the following main topics:

- The key messages from the book – specifically, we will look at some underlying root causes of anti-patterns

- How to use anti-patterns in your own architectural practice to improve the quality of the architectures that you create

- How you can go to further your understanding of anti-patterns and develop your own architecture skills

After completing this chapter, you will have a good understanding of how further your own architectural development and know how to integrate antipattern-based thinking in your day-to-day practice as an architect.

Summarizing the key messages

In this book, we have covered dozens of anti-patterns across seven different architectural domains. However, it won't have escaped the perceptive reader that many of the problems and suggested solutions are similar across several different patterns in seemingly different domains.

That indicates that, at a deeper level, anti-patterns have similar root causes that are often due to larger organizational or even psychological factors. Let's look at some of these recurring causes:

- **Wishful thinking**: Several anti-patterns are based on some form of wishful thinking – that is to say, not wanting to confront the technical reality in front of you. In Project Pieism, it is an inability to confront trade-offs and uncertainty; in Golden Hammer, it's an overoptimistic belief in a single tool; and in Unplanned Growth, it's the belief that a solution can be found later. Always be wary of optimism in technical architecture.

- **Systemic blindness**: Many anti-patterns originate in an inability to see the entire system and focusing on a local solution to the detriment of the overall architecture. This includes anti-patterns such as Disconnected Entities, Ignoring the Ecosystem, and Using Packages to Create Silos, and more could be added. Forgetting about the overall sociotechnical system that you are working inside is a sure way to end up with anti-patterns.

- **Replacing a simpler problem with the real problem**: Quite a few anti-patterns originate in a wish to make things simple. Many architectural problems are wicked and allow only for solutions that are imperfect and highly complex. Often, that is not entirely satisfactory to stakeholders who cry out for an easy-to-understand answer, the giving of which often leads to an anti-pattern. Compliant Means Secure and Declarative Means Safe are two examples in the security domain, where we substitute a simple answer for a complex reality. But also, anti-patterns such as MINO, Assumption Driven Customization, and Big Bang Release have much of their background in this factor.

- **Organizational constraints**: Another very common underlying cause of anti-patterns is working to the constraints given by the current organizational setup you find yourself in. Whether it is because of silos within the organization, bad relations with vendors, or political games, the place in which you find yourself organizationally can sometimes lead or even force you down the path of an anti-pattern. This is true for anti-patterns such as Automation Bonanza and Stovepipe, and this is a secondary factor for many other anti-patterns.

- **Weak technical governance**: A lack of effective technical governance is another common cause of anti-patterns. When you don't have any architectural authority or clear standards or conventions, you often get drift that results in anti-patterns. This includes many patterns, such as Intense Coupling, System Proliferation, and Unconstrained Data Synchronization.

- **Lack of discipline**: Finally, a number of anti-patterns boil down to a lack of discipline in the software development life cycle. This includes patterns such as Big Ball of Mud, Spaghetti Sharing Model, Fat Interface, and Dummy Unit Tests, among others. These are, to some extent, the simplest to deal with as the solutions are obvious, but the underlying pressures that drive teams towards taking the easy road can be much harder to deal with.

Looking at the underlying reasons why anti-patterns occur and finding the kinds of patterns that can explain many different ways in which projects go wrong is one of the most fruitful uses of anti-patterns.

We will now proceed to look at how you more concretely can use anti-patterns in practice to improve your architecture skills.

Explaining how to use anti-patterns in practice

If you've gone through this book cover to cover, you will have encountered a large number of patterns for how things can go wrong on a Salesforce project. We have structured this by architecture domain to facilitate your understanding and give you more context.

However, you may still be left with some questions about how to best go about applying this new storehouse of knowledge in your day-to-day work. We propose that there are two main ways in which you can proactively use your knowledge of anti-patterns to improve your architecture practice and hone your architecture skills:

- First, you can use it constructively as part of your architecture and design process
- Second, you can use it diagnostically as part of your approach to understanding architectures designed by others

We will now go through each of these alternatives in the following sections.

Using anti-patterns constructively

Using anti-patterns constructively means that you incorporate antipattern-based thinking in your normal architectural process. There are several ways you can do this from simply having a mental checklist of common anti-patterns that you validate your work against to a systematic check against all the anti-patterns that apply to the current stage of your architecture process.

We recommend a halfway house between these two extremes where you do the following:

1. At the beginning of your architecture process, you make an assessment against the six factors mentioned in the previous section. For each factor rate your environment for how much it is likely to impact your work on a standard 1-5 scale.

2. For all the factors you've rated 4 or 5 on the assessment, compile a list of the various anti-patterns that could potentially happen in your environment. Not all anti-patterns are applicable across the board, so be selective.

3. For those anti-patterns you have selected, make a check both during the initial design and regularly throughout the project to see if they are starting to occur.

4. If you start to see a drift towards a certain anti-pattern, take proactive steps as indicated under the *Better solutions* part of the pattern description.

That way, you are likely to catch the most common anti-patterns well before they manage to make their way into your solution. This approach works fine when you are in charge of the architecture, but what do you do when faced with an existing architecture? We will explore this next.

Using anti-patterns diagnostically

When you come into a brownfield environment as an architect, doing an analysis based on anti-patterns to diagnose the health of the existing architecture can be a very fruitful endeavor that we highly recommend. This analysis can inform both your understanding of the strengths and weaknesses of the current environment and also indicate ways in which you may start to refactor it.

We recommend you do the following:

1. Gather information from existing users and team members familiar with the existing environment, particularly the non-functional characteristics that are likely to indicate the presence of an anti-pattern.

2. Based on the information you gather, make a shortlist of potential anti-patterns that may be found in this architecture.

3. Perform a thorough check of the relevant technical artifacts to confirm or refute the presence of each anti-pattern.

4. Based on your findings, start looking at potential mitigations and assess the impact of the work that you have been brought in to do.

Having now covered the day-to-day use of anti-patterns, we will proceed to discuss where you can go from here in adding to your architecture knowledge.

Going further with anti-patterns

While there is much information in this book, obviously your architectural learning journey does not end here. We suggest that there are three pathways you may want to consider going forward:

- Diving deeper into the anti-pattern literature
- Extending your knowledge of Salesforce architecture
- Extending your general architecture knowledge

For each of these areas, we have selected a range of helpful resources that we will cover in the following sections.

Diving deeper into the anti-pattern literature

There are three resources we particularly recommend for getting even deeper into the concept of anti-patterns:

- The original book, *AntiPatterns: Refactoring Software, Architectures, and Projects in Crisis* by Raphael C. Malveau, William J. Brown, Hays W. "Skip" McCormick, and Thomas J. Mowbray. This book, while highly dated, was extremely important in formalizing and popularizing the concept of anti-patterns. Several of the anti-patterns found in this book can be traced back to this one.

- The best overall discussion of anti-patterns, both in general and of specific anti-patterns, can be found on WikiWikiWeb, `https://wiki.c2.com/?AntiPattern`.

- DevIQ has an excellent repository of anti-patterns that discusses many of the common ones that can be found across platforms, `https://deviq.com/antipatterns/antipatterns-overview`.

We will now proceed to look at how you might fruitfully combine knowledge of anti-patterns with deeper knowledge of Salesforce architecture.

Extending your knowledge of Salesforce architecture

One of the best ways to apply your newfound knowledge of Salesforce anti-patterns is to combine it with deeper knowledge of the key Salesforce architecture domains. We recommend the following books for that:

- First, we recommend *Becoming a Salesforce Certified Technical Architect* by Tameem Bahri for anyone that is on the CTA track or might consider it in the future. Like this book, it is structured by the CTA architecture domains and is therefore highly complementary.

- Another very good Salesforce architecture book is the *Salesforce B2C Solution Architect's Handbook* by Mike King.

- For people with a special interest in the data domain, *Salesforce Data Architecture and Management* by Ahsan Zafar is highly recommended.

However, Salesforce architecture is only one aspect to consider. You should also consider extending your general architecture knowledge.

Extending your general architecture knowledge

While anti-patterns are important, we should also strive to improve our knowledge of architecture in general. Here are some resources to do that:

- First, we recommend the *Solutions Architect's Handbook* by Saurabh Shrivastava and Neelanjali Srivastav, which gives a good introduction to many general architecture subjects

- For a general introduction to CRM and its architecture, we recommend *The Art of CRM* by Max Fatouretchi

- Finally, we recommend *Multi-Cloud Architecture and Governance* by Jeroen Mulder to get a good overview of the increasingly common multi-cloud architecture scenario

We have now covered the content of this chapter and the book and will finish with a final summary.

Summary

Well done, you made it! This was the last chapter of the book and you are now an official anti-pattern aficionado.

In this chapter, we have summarized the main points of the book. In particular, we looked at six underlying factors that are common to many anti-patterns and are part of their root causes.

These provide signposts that architects can use to create an awareness of what anti-patterns are likely to occur in a given architectural context and what measures may be taken to mitigate them.

In order to use this knowledge in practice, we outlined two different approaches to incorporating anti-patterns into your architecture process. First, we looked at how to use it constructively for your own architectures and then how to use it diagnostically for examining existing architectures.

Finally, we looked at where you might go from here in order to expand your knowledge further. We outlined three pathways you might take and gave some suggestions for books and other resources.

Anti-patterns is one of the most interesting areas of general architecture because they tell you how things go wrong in repeatable ways. Learning from the mistakes of others is usually a better idea than making all the mistakes yourself and I hope sincerely that reading this book will have made you much less likely to repeat these anti-patterns yourself as well as how to spot them when others in your context are about to make them.

Software systems are important. Organizations rely on them. Users spend much of their working life interacting with them. As architects, we have a responsibility to help avoid the common errors that keep them working less well than they could have done.

Index

C

Center of Excellence (CoE) 37
Certified Technical Architect (CTA) 7
Change Data Capture (CDC) 135
chatty integration anti-pattern 125
  better solutions 129, 130
  example 125-128
  problem 128
  proposed solution 128, 129
  results 129
cognitive overload 156
  better solutions 158
  example 156
  problem 157
  proposed solution 157
  results 158
compliance-centric organizations, patterns
  drift and remediation 49
  structured circumvention 49
Compliant Is Secure
  example 46, 47
  problem 47
  proposed solution 48
  results 49
  solutions 49, 50
continuous delivery (CD) 143
coupling 29
CTA Review Board
  considerations 39
  preparing 79
  preparing, consideration 135, 136

D

data synchronization 74
  Unconstrained Data Synchronization
    anti-pattern 74

Declarative Is Always Safe anti-pattern
  example 50, 51
  problem 51
  proposed solution 52
  results 52, 53
  solutions 53
Disconnected Entities anti-pattern 68
  example 68, 69
  problem 69
  proposed solution 69
  results 70
  solutions 70
document management system (DMS) 84
dummy unit tests anti-pattern 150
  better solutions 152
  example 150, 151
  problem 151
  proposed solution 151
  results 152

E

ecosystem, ignoring 84
  better solutions 87
  problem 85
  proposed solution 86
  results 86
engineering overflow
  automation bonanza 97
  overweight component 100
Enterprise Resource Planning (ERP) 74
error hiding 107
  better solutions 109
  example 107, 108
  problem 108
  proposed solution 109
  results 109
event-driven architecture (EDA) 103, 117

Packt.com

Subscribe to our online digital library for full access to over 7,000 books and videos, as well as industry leading tools to help you plan your personal development and advance your career. For more information, please visit our website.

Why subscribe?

- Spend less time learning and more time coding with practical eBooks and Videos from over 4,000 industry professionals

- Improve your learning with Skill Plans built especially for you

- Get a free eBook or video every month

- Fully searchable for easy access to vital information

- Copy and paste, print, and bookmark content

Did you know that Packt offers eBook versions of every book published, with PDF and ePub files available? You can upgrade to the eBook version at packt.com and as a print book customer, you are entitled to a discount on the eBook copy. Get in touch with us at customercare@packtpub.com for more details.

At www.packt.com, you can also read a collection of free technical articles, sign up for a range of free newsletters, and receive exclusive discounts and offers on Packt books and eBooks.

Other Books You May Enjoy

If you enjoyed this book, you may be interested in these other books by Packt:

Becoming a Salesforce Certified Technical Architect

Tameem Bahri

ISBN: 9781800568754

- Explore data lifecycle management and apply it effectively in the Salesforce ecosystem
- Design appropriate enterprise integration interfaces to build your connected solution
- Understand the essential concepts of identity and access management
- Develop scalable Salesforce data and system architecture
- Design the project environment and release strategy for your solution
- Articulate the benefits, limitations, and design considerations relating to your solution
- Discover tips, tricks, and strategies to prepare for the Salesforce CTA review board exam

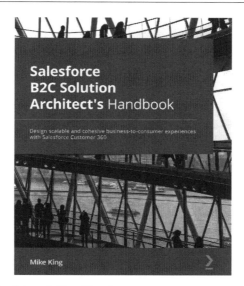

Salesforce B2C Solution Architect's Handbook

Mike King

ISBN: 9781801817035

- Explore key Customer 360 products and their integration options
- Choose the optimum integration architecture to unify data and experiences
- Architect a single view of the customer to support service, marketing, and commerce
- Plan for critical requirements, design decisions, and implementation sequences to avoid sub-optimal solutions
- Integrate Customer 360 solutions into a single-source-of-truth solution such as a master data model
- Support business needs that require functionality from more than one component by orchestrating data and user flows

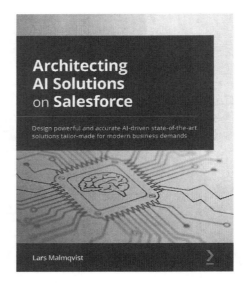

Architecting AI Solutions on Salesforce

Lars Malmqvist

ISBN: 9781801076012

- Explore the Salesforce's AI components and the architectural model for Salesforce Einstein
- Extend the out-of-the-box features using Einstein Services on major Salesforce clouds
- Use Einstein declarative features to create your custom solutions with the right approach
- Design AI solutions on marketing, commerce, and industry clouds
- Use Salesforce Einstein Platform Services APIs to create custom AI solutions
- Integrate third-party AI services such as Microsoft Cognitive Services and Amazon SageMaker into Salesforce

Packt is searching for authors like you

If you're interested in becoming an author for Packt, please visit authors.packtpub.com and apply today. We have worked with thousands of developers and tech professionals, just like you, to help them share their insight with the global tech community. You can make a general application, apply for a specific hot topic that we are recruiting an author for, or submit your own idea.

Share Your Thoughts

Now you've finished *Salesforce Anti-Patterns*, we'd love to hear your thoughts! Scan the QR code below to go straight to the Amazon review page for this book and share your feedback or leave a review on the site that you purchased it from.

https://packt.link/r/1-803-24193-4

Your review is important to us and the tech community and will help us make sure we're delivering excellent quality content.

Download a free PDF copy of this book

Thanks for purchasing this book!

Do you like to read on the go but are unable to carry your print books everywhere?

Is your eBook purchase not compatible with the device of your choice?

Don't worry, now with every Packt book you get a DRM-free PDF version of that book at no cost.

Read anywhere, any place, on any device. Search, copy, and paste code from your favorite technical books directly into your application.

The perks don't stop there, you can get exclusive access to discounts, newsletters, and great free content in your inbox daily

Follow these simple steps to get the benefits:

1. Scan the QR code or visit the link below

https://packt.link/free-ebook/978-1-80324-193-7

2. Submit your proof of purchase
3. That's it! We'll send your free PDF and other benefits to your email directly